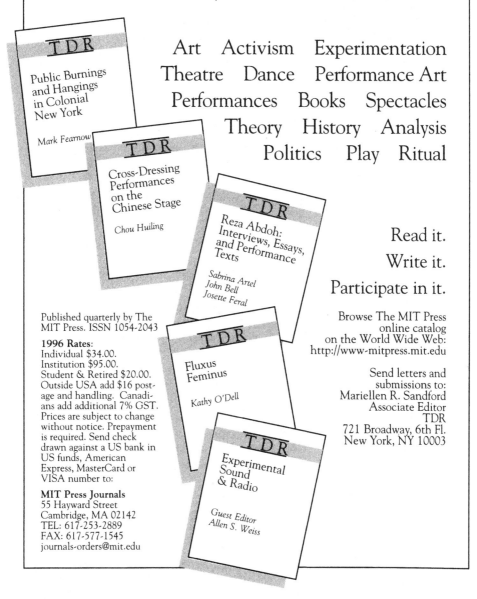

Successor journal to *Theatre Quarterly* (1971–1981)
VOLUME XIII   NUMBER 49   FEBRUARY 1997

Editors
CLIVE BARKER
SIMON TRUSSLER

Advisory Editors: Arthur Ballet, Eugenio Barba, Susan Bassnett,
Tracy Davis, Martin Esslin, Maggie Gale (*Book Reviews Editor*),
Lizbeth Goodman, Peter Hepple, Ian Herbert, Jan Kott,
Brian Murphy, Sarah Stanton, Ian Watson

Contents

*New Theatre Quarterly is published in February, May, August, and November by Cambridge University Press, The Edinburgh
Building, Shaftesbury Road, Cambridge CB2 2RU, England*   ISBN 0 521 58902 9   ISSN 0266 – 464X

CAMBRIDGE
UNIVERSITY PRESS

University Printing House, Cambridge CB2 8BS, United Kingdom

One Liberty Plaza, 20th Floor, New York, NY 10006, USA

477 Williamstown Road, Port Melbourne, VIC 3207, Australia

314-321, 3rd Floor, Plot 3, Splendor Forum, Jasola District Centre, New Delhi - 110025, India

79 Anson Road, #06-04/06, Singapore 079906

Cambridge University Press is part of the University of Cambridge.

It furthers the University's mission by disseminating knowledge in the pursuit of education, learning and research at the highest international levels of excellence.

www.cambridge.org
Information on this title: www.cambridge.org/9780521589024

© Cambridge University Press 1997

A catalogue record for this publication is available from the British Library

ISBN 978-0-521-58902-4 Paperback

Subscriptions
New Theatre Quarterly (ISSN: 0266-464X) is published quarterly by Cambridge University Press, The Edinburgh Building, Shaftesbury Road, Cambridge CB2 2RU, UK, and The Journals Department, 40 West 20th Street, New York, NY 10011-4211, USA.

Four parts form a volume. The subscription price, which includes postage (excluding VAT), of Volume XIII, 1997, is £47.00 (US$82.00 in the USA, Canada and Mexico) for institutions, £27.00 (US$39.00) for individuals ordering direct from the publishers and certifying that the Journal is for their personal use. Single parts cost £13.00 (US$22.00 in the USA, Canada and Mexico) plus postage. EU subscribers (outside the UK) who are not registered for VAT should add VAT at their country's rate. VAT registered subscribers should provide their VAT registration number. Prices include delivery by air. Japanese prices for institutions are available from Kinokuniya Company Ltd., P.O. Box 55, Chitose, Tokyo 156, Japan.

Orders, which must be accompanied by payment, may be sent to a bookseller or to the publishers (in the USA, Canada and Mexico to the North American Branch). Periodicals postage paid at New York, NY, and at additional mailing offices. POSTMASTER: send address changes in the USA, Canada and Mexico to *New Theatre Quarterly*, Cambridge University Press, The Journals Department, 40 West 20th Street, New York, NY 10011-4211.

Claims for missing issues will only be considered if made immediately on receipt of the following issue.

Information on *New Theatre Quarterly* and all other Cambridge journals can be accessed via http://www.cup.cam.ac.uk/ and in North America via http://www.cup.org/.

Volker Schachenmayr

Emma Lyon, the Attitude, and Goethean Performance Theory

The origins of the *tableau vivant* can be traced back at least to the *pantomimus* of ancient Rome, but the form achieved its peak of modern popularity in the late eighteenth and early nineteenth centuries, when *poses plastiques* sometimes struck an ambiguous balance between art and pornography. In the following article, Volker Schachenmayr calls for a re-evaluation of the form, investigating how far and in what ways a static pose, or *attitude*, can be a theatrical performance. His article focuses on the *attitudes* of Emma Lyon, later and more familiarly known as wife to Sir William Hamilton and mistress to Nelson. Drawing on connections with Sir William's archaeological pursuits, and with the performance theory of Goethe, an admirer of Emma's attitudes, he suggests a vocabulary to make the *tableau* accessible to performance critics, using Goethe's *Italienische Reise* and Poussin's *Inspiration of the Epic Poet* to shape the discussion. Volker Schachenmayr received his PhD in Drama from Stanford University, and this article is part of a larger research project on Winckelmann, the Grand Tour, and stage performance in the age of Goethe.

IN THE YEARS between 1786 and 1791, Emma Lyon, as consort to Sir William Hamilton and a prominent figure among the expatriate community in Naples, developed a style of mute, largely immobile dramatic performance called the *attitude*. Lyon's work enjoyed widespread popularity in the expatriate community in Naples, among the *grand tourists* who saw her, and in the broader European context.

Her *attitudes* resemble the *tableaux vivants* that would sweep Europe in the nineteenth century. As for her own historical moment, Lyon's *attitudes* gained the admiration of the prominent stage theorist and practitioner, Johann Wolfgang Goethe. Goethe believed that Emma Lyon's work was an exciting experiment in the fusion of stage performance and visual art. This article will serve as an introduction to Emma Lyon's work. It provides a brief overview of her artistic activities and then lays the groundwork for a performance theory of the *attitude* by analyzing Goethe's critical response to her performances.

Before Naples, Lyon had been a painter's model and a child prostitute, yet in Naples she performed poses from the most august and refined of classical statuary. As we

study her work, we shall see that her idiosyncratic personal history informs her performance appeal: she portrays classical statuary as both idealized, erotic, and inanimate material. Furthermore, since her husband, Sir William Hamilton, was a renowned archeologist, Emma's *attitudes* were in some ways an extension of his work: he had married one of his statues, or so went popular rumour. We will examine how the performer may attain a state of marble presence, how the classical ideal may be an erotic artifact, and how we may apply these insights to the performance theory of Goethe's Weimar classicism.

The *attitude* style of performance flourished in the last decades of the eighteenth century (see Langen and Holmström), spawning companion movements, such as the monodrama or the *tableau vivant*, which still exist in some form today. In the 1780s through the early 1800s there were several artists performing in this genre: Henriette Hendel-Schütz, Gustav von Seckendorff (pseudonym, Patrick Peale), Ida Brun, and Sophie Schröder all built careers based on static, non-speaking performances (Langen). Emma Lyon's own *attitudes* were essentially static: she would move from one pose to the

3

next, hold it, and after a given period move on to the next. Sometimes she incorporated a narrative or musical component, but such words and sounds always came from a secondary source. Either a narrator would speak or a musician play, but these performers were not visually significant.

These performances still resonate in our day. The *tableau vivant* remains an active performance genre, particularly evident in Cindy Sherman's work. Furthermore, Emma Lyon still enjoys name recognition today, and has appeared as the subject of recent popular biographies. Even Hollywood has told her story: in 1941, Alexander Korda made his Hollywood film debut with a blockbuster called *That Hamilton Woman*, which starred Vivien Leigh as Emma and Laurence Olivier in the male lead. It was not the only film treatment she received: *That Hamilton Woman* had been preceded by *The Divine Lady* (1929) and was to be followed by *The Nelson Affair* (1973).

Youthful Transgressions

Emma Lyon would eventually become Emma, Lady Hamilton, but she was born Emily Lyon in London in April, 1765.[1] She spent her childhood in poverty, most likely earning money as a child prostitute. Her first extended relationship with an aristocrat came in 1781, when Sir Harry Featherstonhaugh brought her to his country estate for the summer. She left Featherstonhaugh's house after he had discovered that she was pregnant.

Around 1780, she found some success as a professional model for portrait artists and other painters. She posed extensively for George Romney (Holmström, p. 129) and his friends; among this group of young men she also made the acquaintance of Charles Greville. Greville was a well-connected but penniless man, who counted Sir William Hamilton, the British envoy in Naples, among his prominent relations, Hamilton being his uncle. Emily then moved in with Greville, who christened her with the more cosmopolitan name of Emma (Fothergill, p. 197); here she set about educating herself

while also fulfilling her role as Greville's companion. Her involvement with Greville would eventually lead to a series of astonishing transgressions over class boundaries that culminated in her marriage to Sir William Hamilton.

Greville introduced Lyon to his uncle when Hamilton came to London on a visit in 1783. The young woman would subsequently become a bargaining chip in friendly negotiations between Sir William, a kindly and wealthy uncle, and Greville, a rakish nephew strapped for cash. Hamilton thus arranged to purchase one of George Romney's paintings of Lyon as a bacchante before he left London: this was to be shipped to Naples, but soon Greville had arranged to send Emma herself – for a price.

The letters between nephew and uncle read as though they were financial negotiations. Emma's passage was arranged in the context of Greville's debt, Lyon's charms, the amount of financial support she would need, and debates as to whether she would cuckold Sir William with *grand tourists* visiting Naples (Fothergill, p. 206-16). In one letter, Greville writes to his uncle, 'At your age a clean and comfortable woman is not superfluous, but I should rather purchase it than acquire it' (p. 209).

Hamilton, although 53 and widowed, agreed to take Emma Lyon. He consented to pay her a stipend of fifty pounds sterling per year (p. 211), and she duly arrived at the Palazzo Sessa, Hamilton's Neapolitan home, on 26 April 1786. Though it had not been Sir William's original intention, the two were married on 6 September 1791.

Lyon's performance activity in this five-year period between 1786 and 1791 is the subject of what follows. Two historical incidents bracket these years and provide the starting point for developing a theoretical dimension to Lyon's work. The first is the correspondence between Greville and Hamilton that led up to Lyon's arrival in Naples. This series of letters actually began with negotiations about an entirely different object, namely George Romney's portrait of Lyon (p. 206). Sending the picture to Naples was a necessary first step in the negotiations that would eventually lead to sending the woman herself. Hamilton's relationship with Lyon would persist in its emphasis on the pictorial. Her function in Sir William's household was consistently to alternate between her physical presence and her easy transition into a static, pictorial space.[2]

The second historical item comes at the end of the five-year period in question. Responding to the news that Hamilton had wed Emma Lyon, Horace Walpole commented in 1791: 'Sir William Hamilton has actually married his Gallery of Statues' (Fothergill, p. 251) – a comment which introduces the topic of William Hamilton's career beyond his ambassadorial duties, namely his role as excavator, collector, and author of books on classical art. Emma Lyon's performances between 1786 and 1791 were intimately linked with her companion's activity as an archeologist. One could argue that she brought about William's marriage proposal by virtue of her efficacy as a performer of *attitudes*, since, while she was in Naples, Emma Lyon focused her poses on a very specific subject matter: she posed as the most treasured artifacts in Hamilton's collection of classical statuary.

Using her example, we will bring together several ideas concerning the classical body in performance: how archeological activity influences theatrical activity, how the human performer may attain statuary presence, and how the plastic and narrative arts overlap in performance.

An idealized drawing of one of Emma Hamilton's attitudes. The urn reinforces the connection between the performance and Sir William's art collection.

Performing the Classical Body

Before she established herself with a group of aristocratic bachelors in the early 1780s, Emma Lyon found employment in London at one point with James Graham (1745-94). Though he had studied medicine briefly and used the title of Doctor, Graham was a quack. He ran a 'Temple of Health' in the Adelphi, an institution which blurred the boundaries between alternative medicine and prostitution. Graham's 'Temple' also offered popular entertainment in the form of lectures and performances. His speeches touched on the healing powers of prayer, meditation,

and oils that he had on sale. Those who wished to cure impotence were invited to experience Graham's 'celestial bed'.

Emma Lyon's first exposure to the genre of the *attitude* came as a result of her employment with Dr. Graham, who, during his presentations, surrounded himself with classical statues and young women who posed in classical *tableaux* (Fothergill, p. 198). Lyon posed as the Goddess of Health during these presentations, which were held in the most exclusive of Graham's rooms, the 'Great Apollo Apartment', which one of his fliers advertised as 'A magnificent temple, sacred to health, and dedicated to Apollo' (Laughton, p. 149). These performances introduced Emma Lyon to the art of performing *attitudes* of classical statuary. Lightly clad and side-by-side with plaster reproductions of well-known statues, Emma Lyon learned the rudiments of a technique she would later polish at Naples.

We have no visual documentation of Emma's performances at Dr. Graham's, but the details of his quack healing philosophies make a connection with the spirit of classicism later to be invoked by Goethe. Graham lectured on vegetarianism, good sleeping habits, and the health-giving benefits of less constrictive clothing (Laughton, p. 149), significantly associating these qualities with the image of the classical body – much as Goethe, some years later, invoked antiquity as the model of health.

In his manifesto for neoclassicism, the essay of 1805, 'Winckelmann und sein Jahrhundert', Goethe describes the healing powers available to the ancient physique. He claims that 'Unglück zu ertragen, waren jene Naturen höchlich geschickt: denn wie die gesunde Faser dem übel wiedersterbt, und bei jedem krankhaften Anfall sich eilig wieder herstellt; so vermag der jenen eigene gesunde Sinn sich gegen innern und äußern Unfall geschwind und leicht wieder herzustellen' (Goethe, 1, 46, p. 23). The very fibre (*Faser*) of the classical body possesses restorative powers to which the eighteenth-century body should aspire.

Emma Lyon's experiences here may not have been aesthetically sophisticated implementations of the classical body such as she would develop later: however, her early work and Goethe's essay share a significant, if simple, point in common: by performing the classical body, one can bring an effective gravity, a 'celestial' aspect to the event. By imitating the fibre of antiquity's statues, the performer is able to elevate her work and evoke awe and wonder from her audience.

As its name announces, Dr. Graham's Temple of Health relied on a vague alternative spirituality combined with classical aesthetics in order to attract ticket sales. When Emma Lyon worked there, her per-

formances would have taken place in a context calculated to elicit inspiration, visual pleasure, and erotic appeal at once. Graham used classical aesthetics in his Great Apollo Apartment in order to support his project through the legitimacy of ancient culture, to suggest a spiritual dimension – and then, finally, to display attractive young women to reinforce the idea that classical health and/or a cure for impotence was attainable. Before the visitor reached the Apollo Apartment, he would pass through an entrance hall decorated with crutches purportedly abandoned by patients who had been healed within.

The Apollo Apartment contained a small classical temple as well as some statuary. Recalling that the entire establishment was called a temple, this second sacred structure would have served as the building's inner core. If we imagine that Dr. Graham stood in front of this inner temple as he lectured, surrounded by a semi-circle of posed young women, his speeches would have appeared to be taking place near the source of healing itself. And Emma Lyon would have served as proof positive that Graham's potions worked: she was a classical statue brought to life, a revitalized antiquity that enshrouded Graham in the eyes of his public.

Lyon's Technique of the Attitude

Dr. Graham's 'Temple' was her first place of regular employment, wherein she was instructed to combine her erotic appeal with classical poses in order to further Graham's business. She then moved into more private domains in order to support herself. First with Featherstonhaugh, then with Greville, she continued her work in paratheatrical forms by taking part in amateur theatricals and posing for portraits. When Hamilton met her in London, he reacted by remarking 'She is finer than anything that is to be found in antique art' (Laughton, p. 149). As part of her commerce with the world, Lyon had learned to cultivate her own appearance in order to effect classical presence.

Emma Lyon performed her *attitudes* in Naples with minimal technical support. Her

Emma Lyon sometimes performed major dramatic roles, albeit silently: above left, her portrayal of Medea, with one of her murdered children. Right: Emma posed as Tamar, David's daughter raped by her brother Amnon.

subject matter ranged from the classical tradition, in which she performed Niobe, Pylades, and Medea, among others, to the Virgin Mary. Yet despite the diversity of her subjects, she needed only a classical robe – a 'drape' – in order to convey the transitions from one subject to the next, each of the poses lasting ten minutes or less (Holmström, p. 116).

We know that some practitioners of the *attitude* accompanied their work with narration and music,[3] but the extent to which this occurred in Emma's case is unclear. Sir William would occasionally explain poses as he narrated the performances, and the audience's reaction to a given pose would also indicate that it was complete and recognizable. Since Lyon would not withdraw behind a curtain between poses, and the costume seldom changed, the performances were fluid events and required the audience to make an effort at identifying the classical statue being imitated. There was something of the pantomime in Emma's work.

Technical support for Lyon's performances was limited to the domain of lighting. Sir William was responsible for this effect. He used torchlight to nuance Lyon's expressions and to attain the ominous effects of silhouette. Reports of her performances note a use of light that was rare at the time: if the performance took place by day, the windows were darkened so that the light came exclusively from Sir William's torch (Holmström, p. 117).

Lyon's use of light echoes a popular trend among *grand tourists* in the 1780s, when tourists and artists visited sculpture gardens and studios by night and illuminated the statuary with torches (p. 117). The spectators aimed to make the statuary seem as though it were alive; by the flickering of the torchlight, the contours of the marble would seem to take on the pulse of live flesh and veins.

Goethe and the Attitude

Goethe arrived in Naples during the Spring of 1787, accompanied by his friend the painter Johann Heinrich Tischbein (1751-1829). When he saw Emma Lyon perform her *attitudes*, he described his experience as follows:

Er hat sie bei sich, eine Engländerin von etwa zwanzig Jahren. Sie ist sehr schön und wohl gebaut. Er hat ihr ein griechisch Gewand machen lassen, das sie trefflich kleidet, dazu löst sie ihre Haare auf, nimmt ein paar Shawls und macht eine Abwechslung von Stellungen, Gebärden, Mienen pp., daß man zuletzt wirklich meint man träume. Man schaut, was so viele tausend Künstler gerne geleistet hätten, hier ganz fertig, in Bewegung und überraschender Abwechslung. Stehend, kniend, sitzend, liegend, ernst, traurig, neckisch, ausschweifend, bußfertig, lockend, drohend, ängstlich pp. eins folgt aufs andere und aus dem andern. Sie weiß zu jedem Ausdruck die Faltern des Schleiers zu wählen, zu wechseln, und macht sich hundert Arten von Kopfputz mit denselben Tüchern. Der alte Ritter hält das Licht dazu und hat mit ganzer Seele sich diesem Gegenstand ergeben. Er findet in ihr alle Antiken, alle schöne Profile der Sicilianischen Münzen, ja den Belveder'schen Apoll selbst. Soviel ist gewiß, der Spaß ist einzig! Wir haben ihn schon zwei Abende genossen. Heute früh malt sie Tischbein.
(Goethe, 1, 31, p. 55)

This rich passage from Goethe's *Italienische Reise* opens up several paths of inquiry. Emma Lyon emerges from this description as the practitioner of an appealing art form: Goethe's passage makes a strong link between Hamilton's activity as an excavator and his pleasure in Emma's performances. The description also mentions her use of the drape to bring about character changes very quickly and simply, and confirms that the performances took place at night with Sir William holding the torch.

The passage also indicates the easy rhythm and dream-like characteristics of Lyon's work: she appears to Goethe to exceed the efforts of thousands of painters who tried to represent the human body. He notes that with Lyon, the picture is 'ganz fertig, in Bewegung und überraschender Abwechslung'. In an odd description of Lyon as if she were the product of a painter's efforts, Goethe announces her the finer painting.

The other major passage in Goethe's *Italienische Reise* devoted to Emma Lyon's performances occurs during his second trip to Naples. After seeing Lyon perform once, Goethe left Naples for Sicily. He returned to Naples again afterwards, staying this time at the Palazzo Sessa, and on this occasion Hamilton showed Goethe the cellars in which his antiquities and various unsorted curiosities were stored. Goethe saw a casket-like box in the cellars which had been used in Lyon's previous performances (Fothergill, p. 233). He describes this container as black on the inside and framed in gold. The piece was large enough for a person: it was explained to Goethe that

Der Kunst- und Mädchenfreund [Hamilton], nicht zufrieden das schöne Gebild als bewegliche Statue zu sehen, wollte sich auch an ihr als an einem bunten, unnachahmbaren Gemälde ergötzen und so hatte sie manchmal innerhalb dieses goldnen Rahmens, auf schwarzem Grund vielfarbig gekleidet, die antiken Gemälde von Pompeji und selbst neuere Meisterwerke nachgeahmt. (Goethe, 1, 31, p. 251)

This frame indicates that Emma Lyon's performances at Naples began as more static events than they would eventually become. The frame also makes clear that when Goethe compared Lyon's work to the work of thousands of painters, the comparison was grounded in the performances which Hamilton had been orchestrating with Lyon. The pictorial dimension of the performances that Goethe hinted at in his first description was the acknowledged aesthetic foundation on which the performances were built.

Movements as Moments of Focus

First, then, Emma Lyon's performances need to be examined on the border between a static, composed visual art form – which I will call the pictorial – and the narrative mode of storytelling. Several points of comparison with other aesthetic debates make themselves available when we engage Lyon's work at this boundary between artistic genres, and specifically I will be concerned with Goethe's essay 'Über Laokoon' (1798).

Goethe suggests that the *Laocoon* is best viewed by torchlight in order to appreciate the statue's latent sense of movement. Above, we noted that Lyon and Hamilton made strategic use of torchlight for the *attitudes*. Several other points in Goethe's essay contribute to a theory of the *attitude*. At root, Goethe seeks to develop a theory of performance in which the performer maintains the integrity of a static and idealized human figure. The performance event then engages that figure in a narrative sequence without compromising the performer's elevated classical presence.

We recall that the eighteenth century's fascination with the *Laocoon* centered on the larger *ut pictura poesis* debate between poetry and painting that originated with Virgil. Goethe wrote 'Über Laokoon' to be used as the first essay in the journal *Propyläen*, the organ of Weimar classicism. Hoping to emphasize the constraint and moderation in the *Laocoon* statue, Goethe argues that a plastic artwork is autonomous and self-sufficient, with no need for literary associations. Diverging from Lessing, who believed that the plastic arts were more limited than the narrative arts and argued for drama as the highest of all, Goethe contends that form alone is sufficient as an aesthetic experience (Flax, 1984, p. 8-9).

Although Goethe's position in the *Laocoon* debate is supportive of the pictorial rather than narrative, his essay also contributes to a theory of performance. In particular, there is one passage where he describes the statue as though it represented the most fruitful moment between two others: 'kurz vorher darf kein Teil des Ganzen sich in dieser Lage befunden haben, kurz hernach muß jeder Teil genötigt sein, diese Lage zu verlassen' (Goethe, 1, 47, p. 107). *Laocoon* thus functions as a short moment of focus. During those moments directly preceding and following the focused instant, the bodies in the group were somehow less interesting to behold. Either they were frantic, disorganized, or in some way less balanced than they are in the artifact as we have it.

Goethe supports *Laocoon*'s static qualities, but he also admires the statue's ability to communicate movement despite the fact that it is immobile. He writes that if one

were to stand in front of the *Laocoon*, close one's eyes, then reopen them, it would seem as if the figures had actually moved: 'Man wird fürchten, indem man die Augen wieder öffnet, die ganze Gruppe verändert zu finden. Ich möchte sagen, wie sie jetzt dasteht, ist sie ein fixierter Blitz, eine Welle, versteinert im Augenblicke, da sie gegen das Ufer anströmt' (Goethe, 1, 47, p. 107).

The statue as Goethe represents it is always fresh and self-renewing despite its static condition. Its stasis tricks the eye's ability to discern movement by seeming to move in those instants when the eye is closed. Deferring the statue's movement out of the realm of the visible and into a moment of sightlessness, Goethe portrays a compelling statue that performs without moving.

We can sum up Goethe's model of how to view the *Laocoon* with the cinematic concept of a film still. When one film still is isolated from its adjacent stills, the image captures a moment full of motion that has been taken out of a continuum. Yet we know that even when a reel of film plays, there are gaps in the motion portrayed from still to still. If the reel were played slowly enough, these gaps would become perceptible to the human eye. Motion has occurred in these gaps, though imperceptible to the eye: if the film is to be effective it requires a momentary 'blink' as we jump from still to still.

Goethe foretells the cinematic phenomenon by suggesting a much slower equivalent, not with thousands of still images, but with one solid statue. The viewer closes his eyes, and when he reopens them he suspects that the statue has moved, although its physical properties remain unchanged. The *Laocoon* communicates movement – it fairly radiates it, in Goethe's description – but it is fixed.

The 'Über Laokoon' essay is most useful to us here for its term *fixierter Blitz*. This term captures the two-dimensional nature of the classical body's effect on the viewer. Though it is an immobile object, the statuary emanates a force as strong as a flash (*Blitz*). A *fixierter Blitz* extends the paradoxical but rewarding notion that light can flash at an unceasing rate. The flash itself is a term we think of as quick and finite: it begins, intensifies, and subsides. However, Goethe's adjectival addition, *fixiert*, denotes an incessant flashing that has no dimmer or brighter luminosity, only the constant, intense quality of light we associate with the term *Blitz*.

To appropriate the *fixierter Blitz* to a performance aesthetic, the simple opposition of terms in the *ut pictura poesis* debate is insufficient. Goethe's *fixierter Blitz* is an example of a static formal property whose emanation is kinetic. The term spans the contradictory ideas that a flash, which is blinding but intermittent, can also be a constant. Goethe's sense of the *Laocoon* divides according to the same counterintuitive characteristics of the *fixierter Blitz*. All static, material dimensions of the object fall under the term *fixiert*, while the figure's content emanates from within as though it were a light from antiquity, a *Blitz*.

We acknowledge that what motion there is in the *Laocoon* group is deferred to a secondary level. Goethe's essay makes clear that some form of movement manifests itself to the viewer, but such movement takes place on a secondary level, while the eye is closed. This secondary motion is truly abstract: it does not manifest itself in discrete visual terms. As an abstraction, the statuary captures movement more beautifully than a moving phenomenon itself could. Deferring to a secondary realm of vision, movement occurs on an abstracted and non-referential level of perception only.

Neil Flax has claimed that Goethe's 'Über Laokoon' essay presents a 'syntactic' order for viewing the statue. He states that, for Goethe, the *Laocoon* 'is a conditional sentence in stone, an occasion to think a grammatical relation and to see it at the same time' (Flax, 1984, p. 10). Flax chooses grammatical terms in order to explain the secondary level on which motion takes place in Goethe's model. The viewer is able to 'think a grammatical relation' because he perceives motion while his eyes are closed. When he opens his eyes, he is looking at a conditional phrase: if it were to be moving, this statue would move as it seemed to move while the eye was closed.

'Fixierter Blitz' and Emma Lyon

While there is no mention in Goethe's 1798 essay of his experience in Lyon's audience in March 1787, there are strong thematic parallels between his journal entry in *Italienische Reise* and the critical essay 'Über Laokoon'. The texts correspond on the issues of motion and stasis. I will make two comparisons.

First there is Goethe's description of Emma Lyon's work, which evokes a hazy, dream-like atmosphere in which facial gestures and body poses alternate in a surreal sequence. When Lyon moves, she 'macht eine Abwechslung von Stellungen, Gebärden, Mienen pp., daß man zuletzt wirklich meint man träume'. When Goethe compares the viewing experience to that of dreaming (*träumen*), he supports the claim that the *Laocoon* is best appreciated on a secondary level, with closed eyes. Literally, then, the viewer's eyes are closed in both the journal entry and the critical essay.

The second point of comparison is the ease with which Emma Lyon takes on different poses. Since she is able to alternate poses and expressions so smoothly, Goethe perceives her performance as a glut of images that need to be focused. He uses no less than twelve descriptive terms to explain her performance, stringing them together in an enthusiastic spurt: 'Stehend, kniend, sitzend, liegend, ernst, traurig, neckisch, ausschweifend, bußfertig, lockend, drohend, ängstlich'. The poses pass over the viewer with great frequency and variation, forcing him to make an effort to focus.

Goethe wrote that he experienced a similar tension between focus and a flow of gestures when he viewed the *Laocoon*. He described the statue as though it represented the most fruitful moment between two others: 'kurz vorher darf kein Teil des Ganzen sich in dieser Lage befunden haben, kurz hernach muß jeder Teil genötigt sein, diese Lage zu verlassen' (Goethe, 1, 47, p. 107). The *Laocoon* focused Goethe's vision on one particular stance, but he believes he perceived the statue in several other stances. The statue's paradoxical quality of latent movement allows Goethe to see the preceding and following stances; these adjacent stances are then blocked out once he is able to focus on the *Laocoon* as we know it.

Emma Lyon appears in *Italienische Reise* as the manifestation of one pose among many; again, Goethe needs to make an effort at focusing in order to bring her out of the implied haze of a dream. Emma Lyon samples through a series of expressions, and holds certain ones for extended periods. Yet as I stated when I described the details of her performance, it is never patently clear when her pose has actually begun or ended. We cannot be sure if a pose begins once the performer has ceased to move or ends when she resumes movement. Just as the *Laocoon* struck Goethe with the power of latent movement, so Emma Lyon unsettles the viewer's perception by making him question one discrete unit, the pose, among many.

Next, we may compare those passages in Goethe's essay that draw a direct comparison between Lyon's *attitudes* and painting. Goethe describes the performances as a manifestation of a high goal that thousands of painters aspire to, but cannot achieve. His admiration for Emma Lyon's achievement is based on the three criteria of completion, variation, and movement. Comparing her performance to a painter's work, Goethe writes: 'Man schaut, was so viele tausend Künstler gerne geleistet hätten, hier ganz fertig, in Bewegung und überraschender Abwechslung'.

In order to glean as much as possible from Goethe's comparison, we should recall the pictorial aspects of Lyon's performances. She often took the themes of her poses from ancient murals, renaissance paintings, or classical statuary. Furthermore, Emma Lyon had been a professional painter's model before becoming Charles Greville's companion. The subjects of her performances in addition to her own professional background make clear that the performance event was close to a *tableau vivant*. The *tableau* genre is useful to us here because it foregrounds the painterly aspects of performance. Though Lyon's performance was too varied, improvisational, and bare to be called a *tableau*, the term does explain why Goethe would compare the event he witnessed in Naples to a painter's endeavour.

Goethe uses three criteria to compare Lyon's work to a painter's: completion, variation, and movement. As I discuss these three criteria below, it will soon become apparent that the terms contradict each other. It is important to realize that these three terms exist in tension, because (as with the *Laocoon)* Goethe describes the aesthetic moment as if it existed on the paradoxical threshold of both movement and stasis. After I have examined all three of these criteria, it will become clear that the Lyon experience is paradoxically both static and dynamic – in effect, the performer has the effect of radiating.

First Criterion: Completion

First, Goethe claims that Lyon's performances attain completion. They are *ganz fertig*. This comment implies that most painters are unable to evoke the total presence of a human figure in their work, but that Emma Lyon is able to do so in hers. She is literally able to embody those figures that she represents on stage while a painter attempts to represent the human form on canvas with pigments. The question of embodiment in performance, however, is decidedly more complicated than simply having the actor's body physically present on stage and calling it total embodiment.

Twentieth-century performance studies have been preoccupied with the notion of embodiment since Brecht, and today, with the advent of virtual reality, the debate is even more intense. The eighteenth century also showed some concern for these questions. For instance, Joseph Roach presents two opposing schools of acting in the later part of the century. One camp believed that acting was a mechanical task, so that emotions have no real existence apart from their physiological manifestations (Roach, p. 84). The opposing camp endorsed a vitalist philosophy of acting, arguing that the performer's body contains a 'mine' of emotions within it. To act was to 'spring' this mine

(Roach, p. 96) and free a narrative that was embedded within the body.

The debate between the mechanical and the vitalist theories of acting gives one context in which to locate Emma Lyon's work. Goethe, for instance, would have been firmly allied with the mechanical school if we take his 'Regeln für Schauspieler' (1803) as indicative of his theatrical practice. There, he dictates the stance the actor must take whenever on stage, and goes so far as to suggest the precise way he should arrange his fingers: 'At Weimar the actor danced to the *regisseur's* tune . . . pressing his body into kinesthetic templates fashioned for him by the director' (Roach, p. 167).

Lyon's work, however, stands slightly outside the mechanical/vitalist debate because her performances were mute. The emotions she represented were purely gestural and the subject matter she chose was not only based on specific historical and mythological characters, but precise moments in those character's lives. Lyon did not have any narrative sequence within which to develop an emotion and then perform it, nor was she working with a contemporary playwright's rendition of a classical event. Her poses were prescribed by iconographic precedent and as a subset of that precedent her emotional gestures were prescribed as well.

Second Criterion: Variation

In order for us to analyze the question of embodiment in Emma Lyon's performances, Goethe's criterion of completion needs to be considered together with a second criterion he mentions in the same sentence, variation. Goethe admires the *überraschende Abwechslung* in Lyon's work, the ease with which she varied her poses. These frequent, accomplished variations place in doubt whether any of her given poses could be said to be complete. Goethe's descriptive term, *ganz fertig*, implies that each pose attains fulfilment and stasis. Further, Goethe's prioritizing of the *attitude* over a painting suggests that, in addition to being complete, the pose was also a moment of total embodiment, usually unavailable to visual artists.

A tension exists in Goethe's description of Lyon's work; he values both the claim to 'complete' embodiment as well as the pleasing variations the performer is able to effect. Holmström's account of the performances states that Lyon held her *attitudes* for ten minutes (p. 116). However, Goethe's description of his two evenings in Naples with Tischbein suggests a more frequent variation between *attitudes*. The exact rate of variation is not worth dwelling on here; instead, this tension between motion and stasis refers us back to Goethe's 'Über Laokoon', in which he aestheticized a similar tension between two states of movement. We recall Goethe's belief that, on viewing the *Laocoon*, the statue moved while his eyes were closed. Though the statue was immobile when he opened his eyes, it seemed to quiver before him, pushing past the boundary of immobility.

Our analysis of Emma Lyon's work also benefits from a tension felt around the boundary of immobility. Though it would be difficult for her body to attain the composure and balance of a composition in stone, her performances still trick the human eye by blurring the distinction between one *attitude* and the next. Since there is no way of locating the precise coordinates of one single and discrete *attitude* among her movements, a latent sense of motion pervades her body even when it comes to rest.

This perspective on Lyon's performances also has a retroactive effect. The boundaries between immobility and variation are most vague when Lyon is placing the final touches on a given *attitude*; the viewer is unsure when the discrete unit of the *attitude* has begun. However, Lyon's transition out of the *attitude* must have been obvious. She would break out of one *attitude* and start the longer process of arranging her costume and body for the next *attitude*. As she emerges out of one *attitude*, Lyon demarcates it as complete since it is now past. However, the viewer may well have been focusing on the fine-tuning and adjusting that Lyon had been engaging before the break. Retroactively, Lyon accomplishes total embodiment, but no one was aware of this achievement until it had passed.

Emma Lyon's poses wavered in and out of the categories of completion and variation. Better to grasp these mutual terms, Goethe's words on the *Laocoon* are useful. In his essay, he wrote that he perceived the statue's motion while his eyes were closed. When he reopened them, he saw a static object before him that seemed to have moved. I am suggesting the inverse of Goethe's *Laocoon* model for Emma Lyon's work. In her case, the viewer knows that she has just completed a pose when she moves out of it.

Just as Goethe never experienced the *Laocoon*'s movement, Lyon's spectators never see her attain full completion in a single pose; the human body cannot attain such composure. But since her subjects were very often statues or paintings, and she performed in the context of archeology, her work aspired to immobility. She was able to achieve this in a secondary, implied, and retroactive fashion. Always moving but sometimes appearing static, Lyon shared the characteristics that Goethe so admired in the *Laocoon*: the overlap between categories of movement and stasis. The body that occupies those overlapped states of being radiates.

Third Criterion: Movement

In Goethe's last descriptive criterion, movement (*Bewegung*), Emma Lyon's work seems irreconcilable with painting. Goethe supplements his first claim, that the figure is complete, with the additional praise that it can actually move and maintain its completeness: 'Man schaut, was so viele tausend Künstler gerne geleistet hätten, hier ganz fertig, in Bewegung.' The criterion of movement is the most tangible distinction we have encountered so far between the *attitude* and the painting. The first two of Goethe's standards, completion and variation, were applicable to both the plastic arts and theatrical performances. Movement, however, is not available to painting.

Despite the limitations that painting faces, Goethe's admiration of Emma Lyon's *Bewegung* appears in the puzzling context of painting. Why would Goethe compare Lyon's work to a picture if his comparison is then going to use criteria that painting cannot implement, such as movement? The answer lies in the fact that Goethe's vision for the neoclassical theatre was profoundly rooted in painterly terms. In 'Regeln für Schauspieler', he writes that, 'Das Theater ist als ein figurenloses Tableau anzusehen, worin der Schauspieler die Staffage macht' (Goethe, 1, 40, p. 428). By thus referring to the actor as the *staffage* of the picture, as the 'accessory' within it, Goethe underemphasizes the fact that the performer has movement at his disposal in order to endorse the human being's function as part of a pictorial composition.

Goethe states that Emma Lyon is able to achieve a painterly presence, yet she also brings movement to her work. His critical model seeks first to foreground the painterly aspects of the performer's presence on stage and then, once the performer has become pictorialized, Goethe admires her ability to move despite this complete visual embodiment. Movement alone, then, is not a quality that Goethe admires in performances of any genre. Confronted with the spectacle of a *commedia dell'arte* troupe performing improvisations of acrobatic intensity, their agility would not impress Goethe because the performance had not been sufficiently framed within a pictorial context.

Poussin's Style as an Ideal for Performance

In his conception of the theatre, Goethe believed that actors should aspire to a static physical presence on stage, as though they were part of a painterly composition. And such pictorial characteristics extended to all aspects of their lives. For instance, his rules for actors give the following advice on their comportment, even outside the theatre: 'wenn er für sich, oder mit seines gleichen beim essen zu Tische sitzt, soll er immer suchen ein Bild zu formieren, alles mit einer gewissen Grace anfassen, niederstellen pp als wenn es auf der Bühne geschähe, und so immer malerisch darstellen' (Goethe, 1, 40, p. 166).

The movements of the human body should strive to form a picture. By maintaining this graceful comportment, the actor contributes to the theatrical effect that he prized most: the ability to transform the stage into a painting. In the stage directions to his 1808 drama, *Pandora*, Goethe wrote that the stage should be 'im großen Styl nach Poussinischer Weise gedacht' (Goethe, 1, 50, p. 296). Concerning the drama *Proserpina*, Goethe wrote in 1815 that, again, Poussin should serve as the stage designer's example.

Nicolas Poussin (1594-1665), whose work stands at the point of transition from the baroque to classicism, was central to Goethe's vision of stage design. Poussin's heroic landscapes were a model to which the theatre artist should aspire, 'dieser Künstler ist es, welcher dem Dekorateur [Bühnenbildner] im landschaftlichen und architektonischen Fache die herrlichsten Motive darbietet' (Goethe, 1, 40, p. 116). Goethe's 'Rules' make clear that the actor should envision himself in a painted composition; this larger composition, furthermore, should be specifically based on Poussin's classical discipline.

Goethe compared Emma Lyon's work to a painting using three criteria. With his term 'completion', he claimed that Lyon's performance was able fully to embody the representation of the human form on stage, making it *ganz fertig*. Above, I analyzed Goethe's use of the term *überraschende Abwechslung* (variation). I concluded that when these first two criteria are taken together, Lyon is only able to attain total embodiment retroactively because *Abwechslung* unsettles the viewer's ability to distinguish between movement and stasis. There is no discrete unit of the *attitude* in Emma Lyon's work except for the moment after she has broken out of a pose.

Finally, Goethe uses the term *Bewegung* (movement) in order to compare Lyon's work to painting. This last criterion, seemingly unavailable to painting as an artistic genre in the first place, led us to consider Goethe's view on the mutual relationship between stage performance and painting. Though the above references to critical writings by Goethe make clear that the stage

event should be a composed and classical visual phenomenon, we need to expand the precise role of movement within this static, visual domain.

Goethe's three criteria overlap and also contradict each other at points. Complete embodiment and variation, for instance, do not appear to be compatible terms. However, if we consider these three criteria as a triangular model within which to contain the Lyon *attitudes*, the classical body in performance emerges as a specific type of performance event. Returning now to the notion of the *fixierter Blitz*, we will summarize Goethe's theory of the pose by comparing it to Deleuze's writing on antiquity.

Earlier, I explained the *fixierter Blitz* by comparing it to a film still. We will entertain a cinematic analogy again as we turn to Deleuze, who helps us to arrange Goethe's terms of completion, variation, and movement in a model which we may then apply to performance. Echoing Goethe's notion of completion, he writes that, 'For antiquity, movement refers to intelligible elements, forms or ideas which are themselves eternal and immobile.' Deleuze continues with an observation on what is familiar to us as Goethean movement, which he sees – in a different context – as a

regulated transition from one form to another, that is an order of poses or privileged instants, as in a dance. The forms or ideas are supposed to characterize a period of which they express the quintessence, all the rest of the period being filled by the transition, of no interest in itself, from one form to another. (Deleuze, p. 4-8)

Static Focus as Quintessence

We recognize that although cinema is his ostensible subject, Deleuze's observations are also appropriate for the eighteenth-century *attitude*. His model establishes a hierarchy that ranks completion, what he calls quintessence, over movement. He does not mention variation. Variation has no place in Deleuze's model because he already associates movement with discrete forms: movement does not produce a variation of forms, as in Goethe's model. Form is already

'An idealized group of classical figures set against a landscape' in Nicolas Poussin's painting, *The Inspiration of the Epic Poet, c.* 1630 – 'just such a configuration as Goethe had recommended for the theatre designer to emulate' (Musée du Louvre, Departement des Peintures, Paris).

an 'eternal and immobile' element to which movement refers.

Deleuze is most useful to us in separating the 'quintessential' moment from the less significant realm of movement. His model helps us to see that the classical gesture demands one moment of static focus which then 'achieves' the term quintessence. Such a moment of quintessence then radically re-evaluates all the gestural excess preceding and following the quintessential peak.

The peak moment is intense and splendid, and though the performer attains this peak by movement, she then discards that aspect of her performance because it is useless once the peak is clear. When the viewer makes the resounding realization that the performer has arrived at the quintessential pose, the peak – or *Ganzheit*, as Goethe calls it – all other gesture becomes comparatively insignificant. What was earlier a sea of gestures that overwhelmed the viewer and confused the boundaries between one pose and the next comes sharply into focus.

Such ranking occurs in several other writings by Goethe. For instance, he repeats the idea of the *fixierter Blitz* when he describes a classical relief that represents an ancient dancer: 'Die schöne Beweglichkeit der Übergänge . . . ist hier für einen Moment fixiert, so daß wir das Vergangene, Gegenwärtige und Zukünftige zugleich erblicken und schon dadurch in einen überirdischen Zustand verstezt werden' (Goethe, 1, 48, p. 144). The peak moment is *fixiert* and, as in Deleuze's model, the event gains access to a frozen moment isolated from the space in which the performance began.

The dancer in the relief also refers back to another fundamental precept in neoclassical performance: that the climax disrupts time measurements and exists in a realm beyond the traditional categories of past, present, or future. It follows then that Goethe should approve of the manner in which the viewer may 'das Vergangene, Gegenwärtige und Zukünftige zugleich erblicken', while viewing the relief cited above. By observing the performer's body at the static climax, the viewer enters 'dadurch in einen überirdischen Zustand', a continuum that contains past and future within it.

Instead of regarding this supermundane realm as the site of both past and present, we should think of it as a space in which temporal distinctions do not apply. When Goethe claims to glimpse past, present, and future in the dancer, he is describing the absence of time, not three distinct temporal categories. When the performer succeeds in evoking an unearthly sphere, the climactic moment exists in isolation from its gestural context. The peak dismisses the notions of transition or evolution in favour of one awesome *Augenblick*. Kiefer uses the term *plastische Semiosis* to discuss this moment of isolated splendour; it is a dramatic effect that Goethe endorsed at several points in his career (Kiefer, p. 266-82).

We turn now to a comparison between a painting by Poussin and Emma Lyon's work. To conclude our discussion of the *fixierter Blitz* in Goethe's theoretical writings, let us consider Goethe's description of a Pompeiian fresco as his exhortation to the neoclassical stage performer. Just as the painted figures do, so should the performer

aspire 'die augenblicklichen Bewegungen aufzufassen, das Verschwindende festzuhalten, ein Vorhergehendes und Nachfolgendes simultan vorzustellen' (Goethe, 1, 49, p. 176). The classical form captured in a single instant will in turn allow the viewer into an exhilarating, infinite domain.

The Inspiration of the Epic Poet

Poussin's *Inspiration of the Epic Poet* (see previous page) gives us the opportunity to see an idealized group of classical figures set against a landscape. The painting (*c.* 1630) one of Poussin's major works, is just such a configuration as Goethe had recommended for the theatre designer to emulate.

The painting shows a group of three figures surrounded by *putti*. Calliope, the muse of epic poetry and eloquence, stands at the left of the painting; Apollo is seated in the centre with his right arm resting on a lyre. Both figures look right to the anonymous poet, who holds a quill and paper. The poet's eyes are directed upwards, toward a *putto* bearing laurel wreaths. Three volumes of epic poetry, the *Odyssey*, *Iliad*, and *Aeneid*, appear near the bottom of the painting. Two are strewn at Apollo's feet, and a *putto* holds the third volume in his hand.

We know of Goethe's interest in Poussin; by analyzing one of the artist's paintings, we will be able to extend the terms of Goethe's passage in *Italienische Reise* in which he compares Emma Lyon's work to painting. Both the painting and the performance stand out even in their own disciplines as exceptionally static. Secondly, this static event is in both cases intensely dynamic and vibrant. Despite the lack of motion, both pieces exhilarate a given viewer.

Emma Lyon's *attitudes* recall Poussin's painting if we consider Lyon and Calliope as analogous figures. Since Lyon often posed as one of the muses, the first parallel is in the works' similar subject matter. Also, the painting is remarkably static for a scene of apotheosis. Yet just as is evident from Goethe's description of Emma Lyon's performances, immobility is in both cases an occasion for intense confrontation between the classical ideal and those who view it. Both performance and painting allow a moment of exhilaration and communion to occur between a classical body and her eager viewer.

Secondly, both painting and performance utilize the classical drape. Both pieces connect the drape with a specific light source that plays off the drapery to calculated effect. Calliope is the figure in closest proximity to what Verdi (p. 176) calls a 'caressing light' in the painting. Emma Lyon also engages a strong light source – sometimes a torch – in her work. Indeed, we may safely assume that the late eighteenth-century practice of viewing statues at night by torchlight sought to reproduce the luminous effect that Poussin was able to achieve with Calliope.

The drape is the determinant factor in the interplay between human body and light source. Given that neither the Poussin painting nor Lyon's performance show a nude body, it is the drape that communicates the contour of the classical body. The radiant phenomenon of the contour can function as a tactile, transportive, and even biologically living surface. When the drape falls against Calliope's and Emma Lyon's pale skin, the fabric mediates the interaction between light and flesh.

Lastly, the drape is clearly an erotic device. Poussin's painting accents the drape's open and breezy function as clothing by leaving Calliope's left breast exposed. Similarly, Emma Lyon's performances owed no small part of their appeal to the fact that one might glimpse her breast, belly, or thighs while she was performing.

Emma Lyon, erstwhile child prostitute, developed her performances at Naples to incorporate Sir William Hamilton's nearby archeological activity, the late eighteenth-century fascination with antiquity, and – not least – her physical appeal. As such, her *attitudes* were built around a sophisticated balance that incorporated several aesthetic trends of her day. Goethe was drawn to this balance, and he incorporated it in his cutting edge vision for a new style of theatre, a pictorial theatre on the order of a painting by Poussin.

Works Consulted

Deleuze, Gilles, *Cinema 1: the Movement-Image*, trans. Hugh Tomlinson and Barbara Habberjam (London: Athlone, 1986).

Flax, Neil, 'Fiction Wars of Art', *Representations*, VII (1984), p. 1 -25.

———, 'From Portrait to Tableau Vivant: the Pictures of Emilia Galotti', *Eighteenth-Century Studies*, XIX (1985-86), p. 39-55.

Fothergill, Brian, *Sir William Hamilton, Envoy Extraordinary* (London: Faber, 1969).

Goethe, Johann Wolfgang von, *Werke*. 'Sophien-Ausgabe', in 4 sections, 133 volumes (Weimar: Böhlau, 1887-1919).

Holmström, Kirsten Gram, *Monodrama, Attitudes, Tableaux Vivants: Studies on Some Trends of Theatrical Fashion, 1770-1815* (Stockholm: Almquist and Wiksell, 1967).

Kiefer, Klaus H., *Wiedergeburt und neues Leben: Aspekte des Strukturwandels in Goethes Italienischer Reise* (Bonn: Bouvier Verlag Herbert Grundmann, 1978).

Langen, August, 'Attitüde und Tableau in der Goethezeit.' *Jahrbuch der deutschen Schillergesellschaft*, XII (1968), p. 194-258.

Laughton, J. K., 'Lady Hamilton', *Dictionary of National Biography*, XXIV (1890).

Roach, Joseph R., *The Player's Passion* (Newark: University of Delaware Press, 1985).

Verdi, Richard, *Nicolas Poussin, 1594–1665* (London: Zwemmer, 1995).

Notes

1. Until 1791, she used both Hart and Lyon as surnames.

2. An inventory of Hamilton's collection, dated December 1798, reveals fourteen portraits of Emma. For future reference, we should also note that Hamilton owned two paintings by Poussin (Fothergill, p. 298-9).

3. Henriette Hendel-Schütz's work is an example.

Ronald Tavel

Disputing the Canon of American Dramatic 'Literature'

In this article, Ronald Tavel argues that the commercial American theatre, endorsed by the American educational system and theatrical establishment, has never nurtured a vision of the scripted play as art – and has consequently produced no single example of it. The nation's genuine playwrights who saw their tasks as makers of art have, he claims, been neglected throughout American history, and left to wither in the wings. In the 1960s, Ronald Tavel founded and named the still-extant Theatre of The Ridiculous, and has written forty produced plays, a number of which have been translated into a dozen languages and staged in four continents. He has written and directed thirteen films for Andy Warhol: ten of these have recently been restored for international distribution by the New York Museum of Modern Art, and all are to be collected for publication later this year by Sun and Moon Press, Los Angeles. Ronald Tavel lives in Taipei, but is currently teaching a course on Warhol and the filmmaker-architect Jack Smith at the Art Centre College of Design in California. The American Institute in Taiwan selected the article which follows as the keynote address at the Seventeenth Annual Convention of the American Studies Association of the Republic of China.

BACK IN MY COLLEGE DAYS, Professor William Gerhardt, Department of Philosophy, increasingly irked by a student in the last row who insisted upon conversing with her neighbour, class after class, during his lectures, suddenly snapped: 'Excuse me, Miss Delacourt, what is your major?'

'American Literature!' the chatterbox, a shade puffy, announced. 'Oh?' Dr. Gerhardt responded, 'I didn't know there was such a thing.' 'Really, Professor!' returned the indignant young woman: 'What do you call *Moby Dick* – a fish story?'

Without a moment's hesitation, and smiling all the while, Dr. Gerhardt replied, 'Well, the way I heard it, *Moby Dick* is an allegory. Allegory being the lowest form of literature, since it imposes meaning on its subject as opposed to allowing it to emerge organically, and out of necessity, from the material – yes, Miss Delacourt – if you will, a fish story. . . . '

Regardless of how one views American fiction, film, or poetry, is it ever literature – that is, does any vision discovered there since 1620 raise *and answer* the questions, who am I? (as an individual), what am I? (in

and as my species: in its definition as 'the possibility of possibilities'), where am I? (the quantum mechanical posit), and what is my relationship to ultimate reality? – the conscionable must at least pause if and when they turn their sights on American drama.

To be precise, does any work in the conventional canon of American theatrical writing, as studied in universities from sea to shining sea, qualify as literature – at least as our professorial continental counterparts define it? Dr. Gerhardt may have spoken a bit in advance of William Burroughs,[1] and not have tarried long enough with Wallace Stevens, but should he have tolerated with patience or studied with enjoyment the likes of O'Neill, Anderson, Rice, Miller, Wilder, Williams, Inge, Shepard, or Mamet? And if he should not have, how did so sorry a gathering come to collect – how did we accumulate and sanction so questionable, if indeed not inadmissible a (dead) body of work?

Is the case merely, and embarrassingly, that American playwrights are, as a large geographical group, minor in scope, depth, talent, intelligence, and ambition? And that needing material to be studied under the rubric of dramatic writing, so that we can have, secondarily, positions in, and primarily, salaries for, drama departments that the best of the bad has been exhumed and resuscitated? Or does the problem lie elsewhere, with the exhumers and resuscitators, rather than dramatic writers? And if so, how has this academic, not to say civilized, quandary come about?

Some years back the critic assigned to a volume on theatre theory in *The New York Review of Books* took occasion to note the pleasure of his task, since, he claimed, there were really so few books published in the field. Boldly, he went on to speculate as to why that was so, submitting for our discomfiture his considered judgment that, while the American theatre itself has always had its share of highly intelligent practitioners, those who surround, govern, pass on, produce, and reduce for study theatrical work – the artistic directors, reviewers, teachers, critics, legal personnel, investors, promoters, publishers, editors, dramaturgs, anthologists, historians, and so on – are not equally blessed. He thought, in fact, that the least cerebral in academic service turn their attention to drama.

'Plays, after all, are Mickey Mouse', as Michael Feingold once ironied[2] – and inadvertently fingered the compost by then observing that pupils cram drama electives to minimize heady credits, while businessmen, after a tiring meal, fill cushy playhouse seats in order to sleep. In the face of this dollar-backed demand for ease – disguised (for the former as study and the latter culture) and accommodated by uncrowded minds and non-serious souls reviewing new plays and recovering old, by which the canon is established – parades brazen as day the most stubborn and supported case of the Emperor's New Clothes in art: before the footlights of American theatre.

Before turning some attention to the most sacred cows in the canon, and at the risk of vanishing from the press,[3] theatre reviewers should at least be decried if not named: for they have life and death power over plays, and consign them to courtesies or oblivion, deny that as they may. The daunting *New York Times*, from whose evaluation no new work hoping for commercial success ever escapes, thinks nothing, in an age when American plays have never been more American, of appointing foreign reviewers to their first-string position. Can the most carefully trained foreigner ever enter into an intimacy with American English that the born American enjoys – or have ticked off the thousands of associations, innuendoes, memories, sorrows, and ecstasies which the American playwright overhears as he composes, and that the best of American actors furnish in their deliveries? I'm only asking.

The daunting *Village Voice*, from whose evaluation no new work hoping for *succès d'estime* escapes, thinks nothing – in an age whose urgencies obligate artists to stasisize contemplation of option and not bury our humanity in programme and action – of consigning persons with political axes to grind to head their ever shrinking theatre section, not only to write the lead review, but to select, dominate, assign, dictate to, and edit their lower-stringers. Shall we, in this conscience, have art or advocation? Learn of our predicament or be polemicized? Given vision or division, man's condition or retro-ethnocentricity, confirmative action, multi-insulturation, political correction, policed thought, and platonic poets-in-exile? I'm only asking.

Williams's Shifting Characters

A Streetcar Named Desire is arguably the most famous American play. Now that time has cocktail-lounged (or parlour-roomed) its so-called 'shocking' aspects, it even appears in 'definitive' anthologies of contemporary American literature, the very ones most frequently used in college courses at home and abroad. What accounts for its popularity? To generalize, Williams's plays are about loneliness: specifically, the loneliness of somewhat off-centered people (read, women or persons who project themselves as women).

Since most Americans answer yes to being lonely and slightly set apart from the crowd, they are most probably embracing with self-congratulation a presupposed mirror image. More to the point, they confuse Elia Kazan's brilliant film version with the play, and the stunningly creative performances of Vivien Leigh and Marlon Brando with the 'characters' Tennessee Williams constructed. The same audiences which claim to love this play are usually disappointed with, not to say bored and bewildered by, seeing it on stage.

What did Williams actually write? A melodrama that about-faces and backtracks on itself. He begins with a deluding, alcoholic nymphomaniac whose indefinitely prolonged intrusion into the happy household of her younger sister, Stella, and brother-in-law, Stanley, degenerates into an iron-willed preoccupation with breaking down their union. Whereupon Stanley sets about to hold his marriage together, as any sane man would: and, one assumes, wins our sympathy in his efforts to exorcise the resourceful menace.

But midway in the play, largely through excluding the scene in which he tells Mitch what he has learned of Blanche's previous semi-demented promiscuity – and, by the way, the exclusion of the even more crucial scene in which he actually does solicit and earn this information – Stanley's centrality is removed, and shifted to, and accepted with relish by, the now straw-clutching Blanche. Furthermore, the two switch characters. Our embattled hero becomes (rather unbelievably) a feelingless villain, while the aggressive antagonist becomes a heroine suddenly struggling for her mind, life, soul, and somehow western civilization (suggested for our purchase as the quaint essence of the effete, pretentious, shallow, and sentimental).

Can such a funny fellow as Stanley be accepted as a systematic sadist and incestuous rapist? Can so silly a quotation of uncredited campy one-liners (picked up in bathhouses and bars) as is the 'character' of Blanche be the serious object of our rooting or a model with which to identify? Had Stella, perhaps, been given reality or personality, these shenanigans might have been entertained to indicate our decline lent through the unborn 'ape' she carries (and

that, admittedly, wouldn't be much); but I doubt this play is saying anything.

Williams's even more anthologized earlier effort, *The Glass Menagerie*, suffers from similar problems. This piece is about fantasy-ridden, self-deluded Amanda and her attempt to find a husband for her awkward daughter. We spend the wordy majority of the opus with Amanda and her memories, dreams, ambitions, and projections, but no sooner does she succeed in drawing Jim, the elusive bird, into her net, than Williams turns the play over to Laura, her daughter, for what proves to be a prolonged and interesting (though sadly dated) conclusion.

In its obituary for Tennessee Williams, the *Village Voice* settled on deciding that in the end he wrote better scenes than plays. While we can't be certain that the obit author knew exactly why, had Williams really anything to communicate in *Menagerie* he should have to have attended to that stressful obligation with Amanda.

A study in production or otherwise of *Cat on a Hot Tin Roof* reveals the same dilemma. Ignoring for the present the insulting depraved dopiness of his half-created Southern assemblage, how can we trust a playwright who consistently and persistently fails to locate his central character? And, by extension, the authorities who, not in the least unnerved by this, crown him in the canon?

The Embarrassments of O'Neill

Before the desperate decision to describe Tennessee Williams as America's greatest playwright (as in, 'Who else is there?'), there was, of course, Eugene O'Neill. In fact, as Williams's 'exoticism' dates, its sham ever more evident even to the slow, some pedagogues, uncomfortable without the Great American Playwright, have begun to urge O'Neill's reinstatement. While a few of his early one-acters are road maps of construction, and some of his expressionistic work still salvageable by the most imaginative young directors, such as 'Gypsy' George Ferencz,[4] the famed later labours, on which his reputation largely rests, should be conceded as national embarrassments.

With a volume of Greek tragedies on one knee and Sigmund Freud on the other, this sad man, incapable of understanding either, whose perspiration not product impresses, struggled to make English sentences and filled a sanitation truck with words: dead words, flat phrases, deaf tones, stuck sounds, trite allusions, sappy images – and repetition. One extrapolates that audiences of his day were hard of hearing, since every point is made not only more slowly than one would have thought humanly possible, but with a frequency most devoted barflies would quantify mercifully improbable. We are told that he elevated the then theatre-going public: where was it before – in the basements of institutions for the retarded?

In fairness, Fredric March and Florence Eldridge made *Long Day's Journey into Night* work the first time around. But no one has been able to since. We commonly proclaim that anything once done theoretically can be repeated. However, this ignores the fact that two magnificent actors can make Sears catalogue sizzle. This doesn't mean it's well written, but at least it isn't a poetry anthology: so why did a playwright, supposedly at the height of his powers, need so extensively to quote everyone else's verse in 'his' work? Did everyone else say it better? O'Neill acknowledges as much: why don't the fathers and fosterers of the canon?

A Fraudulent Americana

Yet no cow is more sacred in the American academy from Junior High on than Thorton Wilder's *Our Town*. It is difficult to understand the continuing need for the preposterous mythology behind this dishonest picture of American small-town life.[5] For it is not only ideally impossible, it is dull; it is not only life as it never was or could be, it is not 'life' at all; and it is not so much that idle reverie many an instructor thinks we should indulge as a dangerously vacuous bourgeois lust for lies – that *will* have blood.

When one remembers that Wilder was homosexual, the play becomes even more inexplicable: for Wilder could never have experienced such a reality or even have

wanted to. We would be kind if we said that his motives in creating this astonishing fabrication were purely venal; and less generous if we saw it as intentional, as a subtle revenge. For when you sentimentalize an audience and the nation to which its radii extend to the unrelenting degree that this daydream does, you not only render that nation incapable of dealing with its own reality, but school it as a threat to the world beyond. Putting aside blatant and pathetically conspicuous propaganda theatre, it is hard to find a playwright who ever acted with less conscience than Wilder did in writing *Our Town*. It is crime on a national scale. In the bank of truth this play has no credit.

However, with time it has inadvertently gathered some ironically 'redeeming' qualities. For one thing, it makes all the more naked the works that perpetuate its hazardous deceit – that is, the 'Americana' of Horton Foote, Beth Henley, and Sam Shepard. For another, it has elicited in some quarters a sharp response. Lanford Wilson's small-town epic, *The Rimers of Eldritch*, confronts it manfully, down to its unexpected and chillingly disappointing hero, Robert Conklin. To be sure, Lanford Wilson eventually took the route of many of the starving and starry-eyed – right to Broadway and Wilder's bandwagon – but we have his early efforts with which to console ourselves. Joel Oppenheimer's gentle western, *The Great American Desert*, a one-acter which covers amazing ground in less than an hour, also may be seen as a welcome corrective to *Our Town*, as could Rochelle Owens's aggressive invention, *Futz*.[6]

If Edward Albee slips by (and thus is slipped into) the canon, it is probably so (because it is) without the fossilizers' seizing grasp of his exact impact on American theatre. Like his counterpart in song, Dylan, Albee has moved from influence to influence (Beckett, Ionesco, Strindberg, Ibsen, Purdy, McCullers, Eliot, etc.) seemingly *sans* ever locating his own centre; and altogether too much of him, including, sadly, the hilarious *American Dream*, has dated. But when Albee brought *Zoo Story* to New York, he was standing straight and tall to remind us that theatre, that tired entertainment, was also an art form – and could and should be so utilized. Dynamically, in the 'sixties he rallied under that banner an entire genera-tion – which has been slow to acknowledge the debt. His continual efforts in the name of innovatory theatre go overlooked, as do his charities in related areas. If he is seen as 'too' serious (as in taking himself 'too' seriously?), it is nevertheless his multipersuasioned long-time seriousness that sentenced him to short shrift – up until, that is, the belated Pulitzer in 1994.

In the 'fifties the reputation of William Inge equalled and even threatened that of Williams and Miller. Today most students don't recognize his name, and that may be just as well. However, I wish to point out that when Hal in *Picnic* tells Madge that if he doesn't claim what is his in this world he will never amount to anything, Inge is rising to a statement at least articulate – an allega-tion that cannot in all good conscience ever be made on behalf of Tennessee Williams.

And Inge's scenario for *Splendour in the Grass*, with its frightening warning about the dangers of inhibiting deep young love, carries some portent to this day. Inge's shortcomings are all too obvious,[7] but I am mystified by his disappearance from scrip-ture in the blinding light of Arthur Miller's adhesive visibility.

The Common Slob as Tragic Hero

If the designation 'square' has been earned by anyone in the canon, it surely is Miller. Harping throughout his career on 'moral' values so uncomplicated as to irritate rather than compel, his plays, like his recent public pronouncements (on dramaturgy), seem the censorious admonitions of a premature dotage. Nor need we endure his guilt over mistreating everyone from mentors to Marilyn.

The charge of campiness has not been levered loudly (yet) at Art Miller, but Mildred Dunnock led us down that prim-rose path with steady Method step and the quaky voice of her definitive, deadpan,

'What happened in Boston, Willy?' and 'It's just like you're on another trip, Willy.'[8] Only the hardest heart could fight back chuckles here. And the 'verse' of the *Bridge*, with its 'daring' kiss? More camp.

Furthermore, Miller shares along with Williams, Inge, Rice, Mamet, and McNally the discouraging claim for our sympathy and identification with unworthy low-to-middlebrows. What can be said for his Common Slob as Tragic Hero? Probably enough already – but his constant appeal to Greek dramas, though he's shown some awareness of how they were assembled, wants demonstration. He has given thought to writing a domestic, even waterfront tragedy: but it is not competent thought, nor is any of it tenable as regards an American equivalent – aesthetically, socially, politically, or even linguistically – of ancient tragedy. He's not even joined O'Neill in under-standing that such an accomplishment, assu-ming it is possible, will cost a writer every-thing short of daily breath itself.[9]

Speaking of hyperventilating, ampheta-mine driven Sam Shepard[10] brought a veneer of chic modernity to playscribbling in order to conceal – as his intro-writer, the poet Michael McClure pointed out[11] – his true subject matter: 'Who is going to get the family barn?' Shepard has almost replaced Tennessee Williams as America's most often produced dramatist. Is it the 'quality' that effusive reviewers once imagined in his pastime (he devotes more effort and energy to acting) that won him this popularity, or its deep-seated sentimentality, misogyny, and classism? McClure states that there is nothing like blond hair, blue eyes, and pure luck to kick off a playwright's career,[12] even when his skills are modest, sense of struc-ture lacking, ideas (as *True West* demon-strates) nowhere in evidence, experiments rather arbitrary, and dialogue excessive.

McClure has referred to Shepard as 'King of Middlebrows', though that laurel must have appeared too consciously dropout or *outré* for the bandwagon carrying those first, very influential judges who instead gave Shepard Obies for baldly badly written and boring pieces like *Chicago* and *Red Cross*. But if the early one-acters which Shepard now disowns (though they at least shared a convivial liberality with their era) now seem tissue-weight, later dis-plays like *Operation Sidewinder* and what sidestepped playwriting after it, should give even his groupies pause.

Mamet – and the Academy Game

David Mamet, Shepard's current replacement in the canon as 'best contemporary', is something of a tough or wise guy in 'verse'. While it is trivial to argue about contained prose masquerading as verse – if a playwright feels that contained prose which he thinks is verse helps him to control his dialogue, leave him to it – it is worth pointing out that a staggering assortment of villains outdoing each other in twist after sometimes predictable twist does not substitute for the metaphysics of action or a critique of the inexpedience of psychic indolence. We cannot come to an idea of the desirable (that which is good) or praxis of a moral cosmos if our attention is ever held (supposedly) in the dog-eat-dog offices of higher finance – in which, he is eager to tell us, Mamet's 'success' evidently traps him. (What was he expecting – *Our Town*?)

However, we may profit, if unintentionally, from Mamet's 'success', for he has won some co-operative allies insisting on respectable standards for his film work. He doesn't hold a candle to the Coen Brothers at their best (*Miller's Crossing*) or to Wayne Wang at his (*Chan is Missing*),[13] or to several lesser known and wisely not 'outspoken' moviemakers, but Mamet does nothing to shorthand Hollywood's current manual.[14] Hope I haven't spoken too soon.

As for those who are to follow Mamet in enjoying canonization these days, legendary critic Michael Smith[15] fumed some cogency in 1991 when he was offered a professorship. 'I won't play that game', he stated, 'I've spent all my life fighting it.'[16] He described the academy game as lining up O'Neill, Williams, Miller, Albee, Shepard, and Mamet as America's major dramatists and then coming up with a secondary list of six (academically, to match the math), the salient qualification for which is the ethnic and minority status of the honoree rather than their impeccable artistry – roughly two African Americans, an Hispanic American, an Asian American, a Native American, and a professionally gay American, with at least three of these being women.

The unspoken here is that there actually are a comfortable dozen American playwrights meriting university scrutiny, all of them great commercial successes, not to say household words, sanctioned by the democratic aggregate and therefore guaranteed in-line, pre-laundered, and accessible. While Albee might pose some problems in the last respect, the quirks in the others, the soothing synthesis goes, have long since been ironed out by unerring scholars, and a consensual breakdown of what they are about or ever will be is readily available in libraries.

The crop of stage-writers since Nixon's resignation has largely appropriated theatrical form (if not to perform themselves and 'perform' themselves) in order to proselytize,[17] with PC credentials, the stuff and substance of their ambition and achievement – making them less threatening even than their predecessors, more easily ground up, and thus still more welcome to the market-minded fun 'n' games.

People have observed that William Blake often fails to appear in college electives, this being justified by his being not properly an 'eighteenth–century' poet and still less a romantic.[18] The real reason, Virginia, is that he is an exceptionally difficult poet, requiring a deal of application in areas that parallel his work, and that no consensus exists as to what his *oeurve*, taken all in all, should be taken as.

A remindful dilemma obtains in contemporary American drama, with its significant activity roughly from 1959 to 1974 nearly a blank in universities internationally. The readiest excuse is that texts of the period are unavailable, and to a large extent this is true[19–] and all the more astonishing since no such time span in American theatre produced so many practising playwrights (the *New York Post* thus recording that over six hundred new playwrights surfaced between 1960 and 1967 in lower Manhattan alone).

To be sure, the era as cultural if not intellectual history receives a contemptuous nod (as also does the American art product of 1909-17). Prestigious national conferences on the 'sixties phenomenon now conclude that its legacy was the Civil Rights movement, the arts (and literature in particular) being scarcely mentioned.[20] The radicalism of the age is unavoidably the major reason for the investigation blackout – and longer 'embarrassing' stretches with obvious success are written out of history in the proverbial 'conspiracy of silence'. Yet we should not minimalize the reading that its theatrical work, aside from being heavily performance-oriented and therefore problematic subsequently to reimagine, is often, at its best, textually daunting.

Making the Judgements

Not to exasperate or break the concentration of the irresponsible here, but the inheritance in question wants the minds for a moment of those who have turned to cultural, archeological, post-colonial, and gender studies.[21] Again, admitting that this age discourages a firm grasp, much less containment and definition, it is amazing how few assays it has registered to date. Necessarily unnamed authorities on the period, privileged eye witnesses with proven (published) objectivity, given commissions to record it in detail, took the same and simultaneous vacations.

And left who to sit in judgment? Let me give you precise instance. Being a judge sitting upon state grants in playwriting, screenwriting, and musicals is a job no one relishes. By the mid 'eighties there were *circa* nine hundred scripts annually entered just in New York State, and close to four hundred submitting hopefuls in Massachusetts. It requires months to evaluate these with good conscience – of doing little else at night but sitting up in bed with binders of dream, of going through, as Kenneth Bernard has said, 'three or four pairs of glasses'.[22] Given how overworked most serious practitioners of and specialists on theatre are, the real question is who, of those truly responsible, has the time to invest in being a dispenser of grants – in encouraging, sustaining, and rewarding the worthy writers? The answer, these days, is evidently very few.

I had some time to spare back then, and thought that serving as a judge might look good on my *résumé* – but I was genuinely curious, too, as to what actually was being written out there (and not just produced), what were the subjects, themes, preoccupations, fears (often, strikingly enough, quite similar in a twelve-month span) of writers I'd have no other way of encountering. So I consented to judge first for the New York State grants, and then a year later for the Massachusetts ones.

Ignoring for the purposes of argument the range, nature, and experiment of their offerings, I found, to be sure, in both instances dramatists of unusual depth, of delightful achievement, of impeccable ambition and on occasion the talent to match it, and two or three geniuses – the number you'd expect to discover in any given art during any given year.[23]

Why, then, are our stages not resplendent with the work of these stargazers? You know that I shall tell you it was the unqualified judges. And beyond them, the unqualified producers – and the unqualified reviewers before whom they tremble. I'm confronting fact when I report that you will never see the plays of our best playwrights, that they will not reach the stage, that they will disappear as if they never existed, and that their authors in all likelihood, assuming they survive the trauma, will enter other fields.

The awards in both cases (I was voted down) were made according to an openly defended affirmative action in the arts, by which it is assumed that a reader can detect the race and ethnic group the playwright 'represents', whether or not the same is female, gay, or paraplegic – and, surprisingly enough, poor and therefore meriting state funds, or wealthy and therefore not (this latter sometimes called 'grants by zoning').

According to the generally accepted analysis of the acclaimed British theorist,

Jonathan Dollimore, that there is no such thing as a 'sensibility',[24] what then does one do with these judging 'standards'? When this voter objected to replacing their evaluation as art as guidepost with that of the political correctness, period, of the scripts (e.g., Tony Kushner's *Angels in America*), he was informed, in no uncertain and rather aggressive terms, that art, as the effete cultural conclusion of Dead White European Males, died along with them – and none too soon.

Suffocating the Genuine

To end on a positive note lest we also send the youthful second-rate in this discipline scouting for greener pastures of receptivity (and even today's Hollywood is emerald in comparison), here's a quick list for reconsideration.

The work of Rochelle Owens has amazing staying power, enhanced by her actual prophetic endowment (which she, in good seeress tradition, denies any control over or understanding of), so that she trades from consciousnesses that predate the public's by decades. She also gains inestimably from the peculiar poetry of her stage imagery and salty dialogue, both quixotic and ever-fresh, elusive and elusively incapable of staling. *String Game* is a kind of webbed or skeletal 'igloo' which a missionary can neither penetrate nor disentangle; *Istanboul* a sensual, medieval suction pad that absorbs strawing the arousals of the repulsive; and *Belch* an African nightmare barnfired into relief through colonial reverse. Her masterpiece, *Chucky's Hunch*, rewards the closest study.[25]

Maria Irene Fornes sends half-baked feminist critics into tailspins trying to classify her as 'essentialist', an 'unconscious feminist', a 'political activist,' etc., because the best of this prolific playwright stands quite apart from mundane and tired-theory academic categories. Traditionalists get egg on their face as well – like Ruby Cohn, confessing to having seen nothing of hers staged[26] – in their attempts to decipher Fornes's reduced dialogue and minimal stage directions, while missing the auteurship of these constructs (Fornes generally directs, designs, dresses, and lights her first productions).

Thus, the heart-breaking *Sarita* is the praxis *par excellence* of costume and space – and, with only Sarita's shawl, the texture of station, arc, and circle. And *Oscar and Bertha,* on her persistent theme of romantic relationships, is life's geometry breathing before us. Her found-pieces, like nineteenth-century pioneer diaries, express not woman's oppression, but the joy of work: 'that it is good to work, period'.[27] Her *Fefu and Her Friends*, endearing as it is arresting, should never be forgotten.

Jeff Weiss, if he can re-create his *That's How the Rent Gets Paid, Parts I and II*, should have it videoed for the model of high entertainment that it is. *A Funny Walk Home* – actually anything but – is a masterclass in audience participation, psychologically shrewd beyond all other auteurships claiming to represent theatre of audience participation. *The International Wrestling Match* travels miles farther than the numerous works anchored by this same image. And, best of all, there ought be a making public of his home performance when a woman misdialled him for a pizza (Weiss had a number a digit off from a nearby pizza parlour, and was subjected as a result to nightly annoyance) to end laughing insanely and insane.

Lanford Wilson's terrifying *Home Free*, an agoraphobic doubly (and deadly) projected displacement as Marshall Mason imagined and mounted it, must always be performed for the chilling warning it is: 'a lesson to whoso can profit from lessons'.[28] Act I of *Gloria and Esperanza*[29] finds the late Julie Bovasso writing in what I can only call a fourth dimension: it's unlike anything outside Burroughs. And the sustained humour of that act's second scene is unmatched in American literature for its intensity, build, and daring length.

Aside from their hip, terse, and muscular dialogue, a number of Murray Mednick's plays (*The Hunter, The Deer Kill*) raise the standard (to which all after must appeal) for a perfect first act. Anthony Ingrazzia's *The Island*, with not-for-profit theatre's most successful   every-syllable-fully-articulated-everybody-talk-at-once (outdoor banquet) scene, has vanished utterly,[30] as also have Donald Brooks's visionary hallucinations, *Xerxes: the Private Life of Jesus Christ* and *Infinity*,[31] and Harry Koutoukas's *Tidy Passions*, with off-off-Broadway's unquestionably greatest single line.[32] And Daryl Chin's thought-provoking deconstructive 'space designs'[33] need periodic revival lest, inadvertently, ignorant fledgling playwrights appear in their endeavours to be pre-1910.

In fact, the suffocating of America's genuine dramatic writers in favour of resuscitating O'Neill, Williams, and company has its most insidious effect on the newcomers, hurled thereby backwards by decades. The above list is only for starters, but none such ever should exclude the American-as-apple-pie legend, Mae West, an early feminist who went successfully after the religious jugular in *Klondike Annie*, the sheer sham of the western in *My Little Chickadee*, the antinomies of social climbing in *Goin' to Town*, historical anti-revisionists in *Catherine Was Great*, and the synthetic *a priori* nature of cause and effect itself in her bawdy folk classic, *Diamond Lil*[34] – an eternal model for apprentice scriptwriters: who always left 'em laughin'.

Notes

1. Norman Mailer has called Burroughs's *Naked Lunch* the only work of genius in American fiction.

2. In a speech given at the Eugene O'Neill Theater Center National Playwrights' Conference, Waterford, Conn., August 1977. Feingold, a senior reviewer at the *Village Voice* and a professor at Yale Drama School, was a dramaturg at that conference. He frequently translates from the French and German, notably the version of *The Threepenny Opera* which starred Sting.

3. Responding to the hatchet job done on his brazen *Man with Three Arms*, Edward Albee published a memorable article in the *New York Sunday Times* in which he devoted a paragraph apiece to the influential newspaper reviewers, skewering each with a deft thrust and leaving him pinned and wriggling on the wall. Predictably, Albee would not be favourably, even charitably, reviewed for years to come. That neglect has been rectified somewhat by his 1994 Pulitzer Prize for *Three Tall Women*. (Lord Byron, reacting to the unfair and personal criticism of his first volume of poems, *Hours of Idleness*, set the standard for these jolly, authorial responses with his classic 'English Bards and Scotch Reviewers'. He, of course, did not exactly vanish thereafter.)

4. Ferencz was given a well-deserved Obie Award for directing for his revival of *The Hairy Ape* in the early 'seventies.

5. Peterborough, New Hampshire, is the actual site libelled under the famed Grovers Corner *nom de guerre*.

6. *The Rimers of Eldritch, The Great American Desert*, and *Futz* can be found in Albert Poland and Bruce Mailman, eds., *The Off-Off-Broadway Book* (New York: Bobbs-Merrill, 1972). My own musical drama, *Boy on the Straight-Back Chair* (Obie Award, 1969), included in Bonnie Marranca, ed., *Word Plays: an Anthology of New American Drama* (New York: PAJ Publications, 1980), was originally entitled *Their Town*. Enough said.

7. It has been remarked of Madge that she is beautiful so everyone can want her, dumb so everyone can have her. And her home town in home truth seems to be largely populated by women, nearly all of whom respond ravenously to a calendar boy's physique with or (preferably) without something above the clavicle. Similar importance, embarrassing today, is given to the centrefold appearance of the leading duo in *Bus Stop*.

8. Preserved, for our eternal delectation, in her filmic reprisal of Linda.

9. We may be rescued from this quandary in the future by American screenwriters: a genuine, or at least competent, idea of (at least, existential) tragedy is sought out and sorted out in *Miller's Crossing* (Coen Bros., 1990).

10. Robert Coe, 'Saga of Sam Shepard', *New York Times Magazine*, 23 November 1980. Quoting Shepard: 'I don't go to the theatre . . . my cultural appetites are kinda narrow. . . . [New York's] not the cultural centre of America. . . . New York's about as provincial as the smallest town in East Texas.' And on Shepard: 'This recluse from the theatrical mainstream has emerged in recent years as the second most produced American playwright in the country (after Tennessee Williams) . . . what [Clive Barnes] called the "disposable" plays of his early career, most of which he finds embarrassing today. . . . In the mid-1960s, Shepard became the drummer for the Holy Modal Rounders, and wrote the first of several rock-influenced plays. The Rounders, basically an 'amphetamine' band, drew Shepard more deeply into drugs – a part of his New York life style and free-form writing habit from the beginning. He escaped the draft in 1965 by pretending to be a heroin addict. In the summer of 1967, Shepard completed his first full-length play, *La Turista*, written in Mexico under the influence of amphetamines. . . . Under the pressures of growing notoriety and an increasing drug problem, Shepard fled New York "for good" in 1970. He began to ascribe most of his "so-called originality" to ignorance. . . . He has not touched drugs or seen the Empire State Building in five years.' New York stage directors often describe a certain type of hyper and superficial emotional and/or word association in scripts as 'amphetamine-drivel'.

11. Conversation with the writer at McClure's hilltop San Francisco home, May 1981.

12. In his 'Introduction' to Shepard's first anthology, which Shepard personally asked him to write (New York: Winter House Press, 1971).

13. *Chan is Missing* (1980) is the very low-budget, handheld-camera, independently-made first film of Wayne (*The Joy Luck Club*) Wang. A search for a cabbie who disappears with a sizable (borrowed) down payment on a private taxi, it develops into an intriguing speculation on epistemology.

14. *House of Games*, which Mamet wrote and directed, must win kudos for its refusal, against all Hollywood protocol, to mitigate the seamy treachery of all its characters. It holds our interest because we do wish to see the betrayed 'heroine' exact her revenge. It drops big points, however, when we get the idea two-thirds on and learn to out-think Mamet; and our 'heroine's' revenge seems, finally, too good to be true.

15. Michael T. Smith, b. 1935, lead reviewer and editor of the Theatre Department, *Village Voice*, 1960-72. His charming and highly influential column was called 'Theatre Journal'. He is also a playwright and novelist.

16. Conversation with the writer at Smith's West Street apartment, New York, June 1991.

17. For courageous exceptions, other than the high-minded but not quite artistically arrived Richard Nelson (*Jungle Coup, Conjuring an Event, The Vienna Notes, The Killing of Yablonski, Scooping*, etc.), see below.

18. This is one of the most wonderful divinations for letting a master slip through the cracks that has come to our attention. Woe to the artist who eludes category.

19. To beg the question, 'Why not (re)publish some?'

20. *The Times Literary Supplement*, London, January 1983, covering the Modern Language Association's (MLA) 1982 convention on 'The Sixties: a Reassessment', reported: 'The panel . . . agree[d] that the main achievement of the 1960s in the United States was the civil rights movement – literature was hardly mentioned.' Aside from the disastrously successful effort to gloss over the real American drama of this period, there has been, among other successful efforts to date, the glossing over of New York's Coffeehouse Poetry movement, academically speaking the last leg of the Beat Generation and generator of the documentably most varied (also arguably the most interesting) verse of the time.

21. Jonathan Dollimore, *Sexual Dissidence: Augustine to Wilde, Freud to Foucault* (Oxford: Oxford University Press, 1991). The book, which any thinker might be proud to have managed, is a case in point. It is marred by the paucity, datedness, and inferiority of too much of the literature it recalls for paradigm. The noted scholar displays his ignorance of 1960s American theatrical literature (and is none too conversant with American fiction of that period) – my point being that it is precisely within this body of work that Dollimore could have found what he needed to strengthen his arguments, clarify his assertions, and pinpoint the advances and progress he otherwise finds wanting.

22. A playwright, novelist, short-story writer, fiction editor, and Professor of English at Long Island University, who served. His plays include, *Night Club, The Moke-Eater, King Humpy, Mary Jane*, and *The Magic Show of Dr. Ma-Gico*.

23. By binding contract, I may not name them: only winners are announced, and I am enjoined to publish no specific disagreement with the choice.

24. Dollimore, op. cit., warily concedes that the only possible sensibility is camp: and only if it is seen as that sensible sensibility dutifully existing to expose and destroy the fraudulent notion of sensibility. One of the scripts in standing for a New York State grant envisioned a highly romantic seascape o'er which the mysterious and ethereal wraith of a *femme fatale* demolished to a man a shipful of lovelorn sailors. It was defeated (by the other judges) for being obviously the work of a super-reactionary, fossilized, yet somehow still breathing, male chauvinist pig. When I insisted that the list of (anonymously submitted) runners-up be read aloud after the votes were taken, the playwright turned out, sure enough, to be a woman. 'All of you owe me a drink!' I inveighed.

25. *Chucky's Hunch* is a chain of unanswered long letters addressed to an ex-wife that are recited to the audience by a middle-aged man. Occasionally, he is interrupted by a woman's monologue on tape. It is best understood if the speaker is entertained as the author's first husband, and if it is remembered that Owens sometimes images a duel all but to the death, as here with the snake and the porcupine, as the precursor to sex. Rochelle Owens has published several books of poetry and two volumes of plays: *Futz and What Came After* and *The Karl Marx Play and Others*.

26. Ruby Cohn, *New American Dramatists: 1960-1980* (London; Basingstoke: Macmillan, 1982). Professor Cohn is known for her work on Beckett, and for this reason perhaps was approached by Macmillan to survey new American playwrights for their 'Modern Dramatists' series, clearly intended as college texts. Besides seldom having seen the performance-oriented plays about which she writes, she has no 'touch' for the era – its tone, intentions, thrust, or flavour – and manages to misconstrue virtually every piece she attempts to interpret.

27. Conversation with the writer at Fornes's Greenwich Village studio, New York, 1983.

28. Under various pen names, Lanford Wilson has dispatched more episodes for popular TV sitcoms and dramas than one could comfortably list. Invariably, in writing manuals for specific TV shows, a script of his is singled out as the model for beginners. The quote is from Richard Burton's translation of *The Thousand Nights and a Night*.

29. Albert Poland and Bruce Mailman, eds., *The Off-Off-Broadway Book* (New York: Bobbs-Merrill, 1972).

30. Ingrazzia made his appearance, largely in the Bowery and off-Bowery theatres, for the most part after mid-1973 – i.e., at the point that audiences and critics were turning their attention away from innovative theatre and towards Hard Rock, Serious Contemporary, the Punk phenomenon in general, and the hi-tech, high-priced restaurants mushrooming in Manhattan. As a result, this accomplished dramatist received little local recognition. Ingrazzia accordingly went to Berlin in the late 1970s, and there enjoyed not only public but state support. He expanded his efforts into radio and thought better of returning to the new theatrical philistinism.

31. Donald Brooks, whose life as actor, striptease artist, hustler, relapsed and reconverted Catholic, set designer, and director reads like nothing so much as a chapter in the grand tradition of the Maudits, earned even less recognition as a playwright than Ingrazzia. In Brooks's *Xerxes*, set on the Deuce (42nd Street) and in the torment one knows it was lived, a pale chiffon and wire angel suddenly flights a tightrope vaulted above the audience from atop a towering tenement on one side of the depraved, honking drag to one on the opposite side. I'd call it the enviable epiphanal moment in American theatre, were it not for an even more reduced, simultaneously heartbreaking and transcendent half-minute in a later Brooks piece, *House on the Pier*, in which a small cardboard cruise liner, its tiny dining area lights blinking, crosses on the simplest of pulleys a Jersey dusk skyline shallow-depth backdrop

not three yards wide. Worth every Broadway play I've ever seen.

32. 'Every twenty-eight days, four hundred people get laid offa work: anybody wanna —— a star?'

33. Daryl Chin, 'An Anti-Manifesto', *The Drama Review*, XXIV, No. 4 (Winter 1983), p. 36. Although the essay degenerates into a plea for government support, I find the 'formalistic, structural, epistemological' concerns discussed admirably sutured into and projected through his work. More 'genuinely' deconstructive and certainly clearer than Richard Forman, Chin, sadly, appears, so far as the public is concerned, to have been a flash in the pan.

34. This play has half-a-dozen cause and effect subplots in manic competition for our attention, but West blocks our ability to concentrate on all or any of them with her distractive frontal assault. Only a handful of stars share so dazzling a repertoire of distracting qualities, which render us helpless before linear intricacy, but West employs hers – intellectual and, of course, verbal as well as physical – to consistent and conscious iconoclastic purpose: she is nothing if not ambitious. The auteur-author-actress did not permit her plays (*Sex, Sextette, Doin' the Bear, Catherine Was Great, Ring Twice, Come Up, Mae Goes West,* etc.) to be published, but *Diamond Lil,* radically abridged, survives as the wonderfully concise film, *She Done Him Wrong* (1933). When the American Conservatory Theatre, San Francisco, sought to revive *Diamond Lil* in the 'eighties, it took them years to locate a script. Then they found a number of different ones and, after piecing them together, felt that the 'original' must have been too long for contemporary taste. Actually, like the Elizabethans, West used different versions and scenes for revivals, or even the same run. Her films for Paramount and Universal (which she scripted and starred in) are: *Night After Night, She Done Him Wrong, I'm No Angel, Belle of the Nineties, Klondike Annie, Go West, Young Man, Goin' to Town, Every Day's a Holiday, My Little Chickadee,* and *The Heat's On. Myra Breckinridge* was for Fox and *Sextette* (based on her play) was an indie.

References

Fornes, Maria Irene, *Plays* (New York: PAJ Publications, 1986). [Contains: *Mud, The Danube, The Conduct of Life,* and *Sarita.*]

Gottried, Martin, *Opening Nights: Theatre Criticism of the Sixties* (New York: Putnam, 1969).

——, *A Theatre Divided: the Postwar American Stage* (Boston: Little, Brown, 1969).

Marranca, Bonnie, ed., *Theatre of the Ridiculous* (New York: PAJ Publications, 1979). [Contains: *The Life of Lady Godiva* (Tavel), *Stage Blood* (Ludlam), *The Magic Show of Dr Ma-Gico* (Bernard).]

——, *Word Plays: New American Drama* (New York: PAJ Publications, 1980). [Includes: *Fefu and Her Friends* (Fornes), *The Vienna Notes* (Nelson), *Boy on the Straight-Back Chair* (Tavel).]

——, *Word Plays 2* (New York: PAJ Publications, 1982). [Includes: *Chucky's Hunch* (Owens).]

Mednick, Murray, Bill Raden, Cheryl Slean, eds., *Best of the West* (Los Angeles: Padua Hills Press, 1991). [Includes: *Oscar and Bertha* (Fornes), *Shatter 'n' Wade* (Mednick).]

Orzel, Nick and Michael Smith, eds. *Eight Plays from Off-Off-Broadway* (New York: Bobbs-Merrill, 1966). [Includes: Wilson, Terry, Oppenheimer, Shepard, Fornes, etc.]

Poland, Albert, and Bruce Mailman, eds. *The Off-Off-Broadway Book: the Plays, People, Theatre* (New York: Bobbs-Merrill, 1972). [Includes: *The Rimers of Eldritch* (Wilson), *The Great American Desert* (Oppenheimer), *Futz* (Owens), *Gloria and Esperanza* (Bovasso), *The Hawk* (Mednick), *The Unseen Hand* (Shepard), *Invocations of a Haunted Mind* (Koutoukas), *Gorilla Queen* (Tavel), *Country Music* (Michael Smith).]

Schroeder, Robert, ed., *The New Underground Theatre* (New York: Bantam Books, 1968.) [Includes: Mednick, Tavel, Owens, Shepard, van Italie, Fornes.]

Smith, Michael, ed., *The Best of Off-Off-Broadway* (New York: Dutton, 1969). [Includes: Tavel, Shepard, Heide.]

Nadine Holdsworth

Good Nights Out: Activating the Audience with 7:84 (England)

John McGrath is recognized as a leading practitioner and theorist of popular and political theatre, in large part due to his work with 7:84 (England) and 7:84 (Scotland), but also through the contributions he has made to the debate surrounding this form of theatre, as summed up in his publication of *A Good Night Out* in 1981 and of *The Bone Won't Break* in 1990. McGrath has also written numerous articles, including those to be found in TQ19, TQ35, and NTQ4, in which he documents the work of the 7:84 companies and discusses the defining characteristics, ideological perspective, and potential for socio-political intervention of political theatre. Here, Nadine Holdsworth looks specifically at the importance of the audience as it related to 7:84 (England) in the 1970s and 1980s, and identifies some of the strategies employed by the company to attract and maintain a radical working-class audience. Nadine Holdsworth lectures in Theatre Studies at De Montfort University and has recently completed her doctoral thesis on McGrath and the 7:84 (England) Company, from which this research is derived. She has also catalogued an extensive archive on the company which is held at Cambridge University.

THE 7:84 COMPANY was formed by John McGrath as a popular, political touring company in 1971, and divided into the separate English and Scottish branches from 1973. These two companies formed the sustained theatrical experiment from which McGrath derived the theories formulated in *A Good Night Out* a decade later. Hence the cultural and political back-drop to this text was located firmly within the context of 1970s Britain – a factor that is crucial to its vision of class politics, of working-class culture, and of theatrical intervention into society. 7:84 emerged from a period of national and international socio-political and counter-cultural events which initiated the politicization of a new generation of theatre workers, and heralded a burgeoning enclave of left-wing political theatre, which included Red Ladder, Foco Novo, and General Will.[1]

The composition and active role of the audience in the performance process was an ideologically determining factor in much of the work conducted by these practitioners, whether the concern was to challenge audience sensibilities, to generate collective identification, or to politicize. A process of cultural democratization and decentrali-

zation (which steadfastly rejected populism) was embarked on, with a concern to attract a new working-class audience for theatre or to take theatre to working-class communities.

Throughout *A Good Night Out* McGrath stressed the importance of choices in relation to cultural practice and argued that the meanings of the devices and conventions adopted in the theatre predominately supported the cultural, economic, and political dominance of the middle class.[2] Thus, he argued that a crucial aspect of working-class engagement in any performance event was the degree to which it became accessible through the codes people were accustomed to receive and decipher in their everyday lives and in the entertainment they pursued.

This article focuses specifically on 7:84 (England) and asks how this aim was mediated through practice. What strategies, in terms of venue, publicity, and marketing, were employed to locate and generate a politically active working-class audience? And could these strategies provide a framing mechanism within which the performance event could be read and performance efficacy initiated?[3] Did the company succeed in attaining a sustained working-class audience or was this simply an idealistic demand that remained neglectful of the complexity of cultural formation, and, in David Edgar's terms, 'peripheral'?[4]

I am concerned with why and how 7:84 (England)'s relationship with its audience was distinctive during the 1970s and early 1980s, and therefore foreground a piece of theatre history which in the current context appears unrepeatable. The rapidly shifting cultural context of the 1980s invalidated and largely curtailed such projects, to the extent that such a policy in 1990s England would be deemed largely unfeasible and inappropriate. The question follows of where political theatre in England is to be located in the latter half of the 1990s.

In retrospect it is clear that the 1970s and early 1980s did provide a context in which political theatre could flourish, as ideological campaigns and resistance were commonplace in the social, industrial, and personal arenas. There was a resurgence of class-based activism, a phenomenon necessitated by economic crisis, high inflation, and rising unemployment. This contradicted the predominant post-war sociological enquiry, which had suggested a move away from the working class as a distinct socio-political entity, characterized by collective identity and class-consciousness, in favour of the individualistic proclivities of the middle class. Instead trade union membership increased throughout the decade and industrial action was witnessed throughout the country during the 'politics of confrontation' era of Edward Heath's government and subsequently in the 'winter of discontent' under James Callaghan's administration.

Labour and Conservative policies were clearly delineated as oppositional agendas, a polarity which has evidently dispersed during the 1980s and 1990s as the parties contend in the domain of centrist politics. These aspects were integral to many oppositional theatre companies that drew on industrial protest and party politics as central stimuli for their work in support of working-class and socialist enquiry. Similarly, the organized resistance and ideological campaigns of feminism, gay liberation,

and anti-racism were placing the personal onto the political agenda, a factor which became increasingly important to political theatre groups as the 1970s progressed.

Theatrically there was a consolidation of the progressiveness initiated in the latter half of the 1960s, which culminated in the abolition of the Lord Chamberlain's censorship in 1968. In the early part of the decade the tone at the Arts Council was generally one of liberal benevolence towards ideological and theatrical experimentation, and there were positive moves towards support for counter-cultural activity and community-based projects, with the emphasis on channelling their creative and often political energy into practical realization. The whole fringe/alternative theatre scene developed to be a major force in the artistic life of the country and to embrace a wide range of activity.[5]

This was the context for the ideas formulated in *A Good Night Out*, which stressed the ideological nature of arts practice, the possibility for theatrical intervention in the political arena, and of identifying a specifically recognizable and recreatable working-class culture. However, almost as McGrath was writing in 1979, the society he presumed as its *raison d'être* was disappearing – a situation which McGrath tried to make retrospective sense of a decade later in *The Bone Won't Break*.

Location and Venue

7:84 began to receive Arts Council funding in this progressive period, and was initially reliant on the circuit of arts centres and university theatres which had emerged to cater for the growth of small-scale touring companies.[6] As the company progressed, a network of alternative cultural venues was developed, often associated with traditional concepts of working-class employment and left-wing activity. For example, the 1977 production of Edgar's *Wreckers* toured to Norwich Labour Club, Gateshead Boilermaker's Club, Wolstanton Miners Welfare Club, and Marston Sports and Social Club. In this manner the company hoped to encourage the participation of the working-class elements of the community. In these venues the audience did not have to enter a traditional theatre building whose use it associated with the alienating cultural inclinations of the middle class, and did not have to negotiate a social ritual with whose conventions it was unfamiliar. The familiarity with the venue also indicated an ownership of the context, and as an extension of this the event taking place within it – a crucial element for the successful mediation of popular theatre practice.[7]

In terms of marketing, 7:84 (England) also strove to pitch its advertising to a specific readership and advertised locally in community papers, in left-wing publications such as The Leveller and the Morning Star, and in regional trades union newsletters. For a more specific example, the company promoted its 1979 production, Bitter Apples, in the programme for a Nottingham Forest versus Liverpool football match, and as an extension of this strove (unsuccessfully) to enhance its popular working-class credentials by involving Brian Clough in the advertising campaign. We can thus see that the theatrical event offered by 7:84 (England) was intended to function as an extension of the everyday working, political, or leisure pursuits of local working-class communities.

The performance space was also meant to function as a framing mechanism, as part of the signification process. The resonance of the ideological transaction sought by the company was highly dependent on the venues targeted for productions. In 1983, 7:84 (England) produced a Peter Cox play entitled Jimmy Riddle, as part of a double bill with Tickertape and V-Signs. The former play dealt with the closure of the British Leyland plant at Speke, and was concerned to explore the destabilizing and demoralizing effects of long-term unemployment.

During the tour the company played Speke's Community Centre, which had never previously witnessed a theatre production, and, with financial assistance from Merseyside Arts, subsidized the tickets so heavily that they were reduced to thirty-five pence each. By manipulating the context, price,

promotion, and subject matter of the event, 7:84 (England) hoped to attract a large audience – not of regular theatregoers – from a community suffering from severe unemployment and social deprivation .

This was supported by community liaison negotiated through the organizers of the event, who recognized the relevance and immediacy of the issues tackled. They appreciated the validation of experience it offered to their community, a sense of identification which was essential to the reception of the performance – as an article in the Speke Independent Press, a newspaper produced by and for the community, makes evident:

Jimmy Riddle, an active trade unionist made redundant from British Leyland and living in Speke, revealed the reality of the father/husband faced with redundancy and the prospect of long-term unemployment. A brilliant play, brilliantly written, and acted out by the lone performer who kept his audience riveted to their seats in appreciation . . . that certainly took powerful acting and drew such comments from those that watched as 'My dad would have really enjoyed that – he should have come too', or 'I wish I had told our kid this was on tonight – he used to work at Leylands – and he hasn't worked since either.'[8]

It is also pertinent to note that less 'alternative' venues such as arts centres and civic halls were often hired by promoters who were, nevertheless, committed to political activism and attracting a new working-class audience. Hence venues which, on the surface, indicated a cultural and ideological slippage were still often central to a radical process of cultural intervention. The targeting of a particular audience for whom the material had a direct relevance was a central politicizing strategy utilized by 7:84 (England), and ensured that many of the venues were temporarily employed as sites of contest, where counter-cultural views could be openly articulated and celebrated.

7:84 (England) and the Labour Movement

7:84 (England) was openly associated with the Labour Movement. This relationship could take the form of financial backing, as with the Six Men of Dorset production in

1984, or could entail individual performances being organized through a trade union, local Labour Party, or trades council. This alliance functioned as both a rhetorical and authenticating convention through which audiences were initially attracted and could subsequently read the performance event.

Another Cox play, *The Garden of England*, concerned with the predicament of striking miners, was toured during the final stages and the aftermath of the 1984-85 miners' strike. This time the venues chosen included Newcastle City Hall, Sheffield City Hall, and Parc and Dare Theatre, Treochy, South Wales. The choice of venue thus authentically framed the action, since localism was employed as a means of promoting a coherent socio-political critique and maximum effectivity.

This was reinforced by the promotion of the events, the Sheffield performance being organized by the city's Labour Party and clearly functioned to demonstrate solidarity with the striking miners. Thus, the *Sheffield Morning Telegraph* reported that the audience included 1,500 striking miners and their families who had been brought in from twelve local pits by volunteer TGWU bus drivers, and that messages of support were read out by the Yorkshire Miners' President, Jack Taylor, and by Norman Buchan, the Labour arts spokesperson, on behalf of Neil Kinnock.[9]

Indeed, the company had established close links with Kinnock, who had a place on the board of directors and, as with *Six Men of Dorset*, was prepared to hold press conferences to announce his support for 7:84 (England) projects. In the current context of a rapidly changing Labour Party distancing itself from the traditional left and political activism as the need to be electable takes precedence, such a direct association with a determinedly left-of-centre theatre company – not to mention open support of industrial action – appears unthinkable.

The company aimed to provide entertainment, 'a good night out', that addressed social issues within an unambiguous left-wing framework. A central objective was to mediate a vision of collective mobilization

through the on-stage events, and directly to implicate the audience in the need for active opposition. This dynamic process was made blatantly apparent in a policy statement, made by McGrath and recurring as part of the programmes for 7:84 (England):

Any theatre that concentrates on 'emotional' plots and does not question the structures that underlie its characters' lives is being political by default. We choose to examine the political issues openly because they shape the reality we all live in. That reality is not static and accepted – it is dynamic and in the process of change. If it is to change in a way that will make living better, then an open, clear analysis is needed. We hope that our kind of theatre can make a contribution to the way the working class decides its own future – and on the way give people some good theatre, some enjoyable music, a few laughs, and a good night out.[10]

The no-nonsense presentation also adhered to McGrath's call for 'directness', as the left-wing ideological perspective through which the performance had been researched, constructed, and presented was foregrounded in all aspects of the performance event.

Politicizing Strategies

7:84 (England) consistently utilized venue displays and programmes as an effective device for signalling an ideological interpretive framework from which the collective spectator was to construct and read the material presented. The programmes incorporated a history of the company and an explanatory text which highlighted the contemporary social, economic, and political implications of the performance.

In the programme for *The Garden of England* there was thus a clear signification process involved in the selection of material. Photographs chosen to depict the miners' strike were at once emotively and politically charged – one photograph depicting five policemen on horses, wearing 'riot gear', brandishing batons, and chasing a lone shirtless figure towards a 'live cable' sign. Poems were included which had been written by striking miners' partners, there was a note from the company which stated

Above: framing the performance. Picture included in the programme for *The Garden of England* depicting mounted policemen in pursuit of a striking miner (photo: John Harris). Right: a scene of violent interrogation in the 7:84 (England) production of Barrie Keeffe's play *Sus* (photo: Syndics of Cambridge University Library).

'We hope that the play is a worthy testament to the courage and determination of all Britain's mining communities',[11] and it was made clear that all the proceeds of the tour would go to the Miners' Hardship Fund, an act of solidarity which had been made possible by the support of the Labour Movement in subsidizing the tour.

This association with a specific practical campaign further endorsed the politicizing mechanism. For example, the 1980 production of Barrie Keeffe's play *Sus* was performed in conjunction with the Scottish campaign against the Criminal Justice Bill which had initiated the discriminatory 'sus' laws, and *Six Men of Dorset*, a play written by Miles Malleson and Harry Brooks in 1934 to mark the centenary of the Tolpuddle Martyrs, was revived and updated in 1984 within the context of increasing trade union repression.

This practice served to accommodate the company's desire to function not only as entertainers, but as consciousness-raisers concerned to stimulate the working class to self-activity. Indeed this continuation of the struggle outside the performance space was often indicated in the programmes by the inclusion of contact addresses for political movements or specific causes. For example, the programme for *Six Men of Dorset* included the address of the National Council for Civil Liberties, which at that time was campaigning against restrictions on the right to strike, and appealing for funds to finance an independent enquiry into the policing of the miners' strike.

The performance techniques used were also fundamental to these activating principles, since they reinforced the dialectical relationship between the audience and the performance event. Although beyond the scope of the present investigation, they included the central performative apparatus of popular theatre; the appropriation of the agitprop tradition of historical and topical documentary; and the employment of the narrative and analytical function of song, which could also work as an empowering form of cultural affirmation and collective celebration. All these devices and more were utilized not only to enable an entertaining 'good night out', but to provide a conceptual performative framework for the successful mediation of an overtly political analysis of society.

Problematic Passivity?

This can lead to accusations of 'patronizing the audience' and 'preaching to the converted', or can signal a failure to represent the complexity of cultural formation, as contradiction and alternative values are disregarded.[12] Critics similarly point to a problematic passivity in the audience as its members are caricatured or manipulated into a false unanimity of response.

This is a complex debate which offers many valid criticisms: however, it does also negate many positive aspects of the 7:84 (England) experience. The company was effectively trying to create a 'members' club' atmosphere which would nourish group identification, commonality, and cultural/political affirmation. It was not seeking 'performative contradiction',[13] a slippage between the performance context and the performance event, but sought cultural and political consensus with a specific target audience. It wanted to attract a regular, committed audience with whom it could develop an ongoing relationship, which did not necessarily need to invoke the negative association of 'preaching to the converted'.

It is also interesting that the charge of 'being patronizing' largely came from highbrow critics and academics, not from amongst the target audience, which was more likely to be supportive of the company's ability to present a culturally relevant subject in an entertaining way, convincing them that the theatre did not only speak to a socio-cultural minority. This practical intervention could also instigate cultural dissemination, as a letter sent to the Arts Council on 16 May 1984 demonstrates:

A couple of years ago, during the Edinburgh Festival, I took my parents to see *One Big Blow*, a play about miners. My father has been a miner all his working life and neither he or my mother had ever been to see a play before. However I coaxed them to come along and we had a marvellous evening. . . . My father and mother who have always thought theatre was a bit highbrow have been to see a few plays since.[14]

Accusations of being patronizing also undermine the spectatorial pleasure that can be gained from having a particular belief or political alignment overtly portrayed in performance, which can ultimately lead to reaffirmed conviction and to confirmation of the need for active opposition to the status quo.

Difficulties arise when an attempt is made to classify audiences in terms of background and class, although evidence does exist which permits an attempt at this type of exploration in relation to 7:84 (England). In 1978 market research was conducted by Mass Observation Ltd., which compared the audiences for three companies – 7:84 (England), Monstrous Regiment, and the Triple Action Theatre Company – and the results, also formulated for the Arts Council, indicated that 7:84 (England) generated an audience, in certain geographical locations, which was not to be found in other areas of professional theatre.

Of the three groups, 7:84 attracted the greatest representation from that section of the population normally severely under-represented in theatre and other arts performances. At Clay Cross 67 per cent of the audience was drawn from a manual worker background (C2, D, E) and 70 per cent finished their formal education at eighteen or earlier, and at Workington the C2, D, E proportion was 37 per cent [with] 40 per cent [having] completed full-time education before they were nineteen.[15]

These were not regular theatregoers: 'Among the Clay Cross audience only 56 per cent had been in the last five years and 48 per cent in the last year.'[16] The study found that 'the 7:84 group played to audiences nearly 60 per cent of whom had known about 7:84 before they learned about the production they were attending, and nearly 40 per cent had seen the group before'.[17] It is evident that the company had a radical impact in attracting a regular working-class audience in certain locations. Of an audience at the Trades Hall Social Club in Workington, 62 per cent had seen 7:84 (England) perform before, while 79 per cent knew about the company.

7:84 (England) was heavily reliant on a network of politicized local contacts for a particular area or venue. Indeed the company held lists of contacts for geographical locations in its files, which listed the political membership or Labour Movement credentials of the individual. Names and addresses would be followed by such affiliations as NUPE, Local Labour Party, Communist Party, or Dockworker.

These contacts would be approached to promote a show in their area, signalling a strong working-class and politically active network for the company. The Mass Observation study found that 46 per cent of 7:84 (England)'s audience learned of the production through friends or relatives and 14 per cent through a movement or organization. This networking was a factor which 7:84 (England) insisted was a positive strategy in

drawing its predominantly under-represented audience:

7:84 has a unique contact network, and its methods of promotion differ significantly from other small-scale touring companies. The relationship with promoters is crucial, we rely on them to ensure our audiences are aware of the company's visit; many of them are activists in the Labour Movement, many are committed to extending theatre to working-class audiences; some are simply theatre lovers who want a share of the arts, and in particular theatre, but happen to live in Cleator Moor, Bootle, or Connah's Quay.[18]

Developing a Relationship

The company also developed a relationship by appealing for practical assistance, actively implementing an essential network of supporters. During the 1983 production of *Spike in the First World War*, a leaflet was thus circulated to the audience requesting help in any capacity – putting up posters, organizing a coach trip. In this way 7:84 (England) directly appealed to its audience on both a personal and political level:

What we now intend to do is send out a mailing to our friends and supporters to keep them in touch with the company and its plans, so that they can help in the promotion by encouraging even bigger working-class audiences. In these days of rampant Thatcherism the alternative arguments need to be put in an entertaining way and reach as many people as possible. We also want to provide a 'good night out' for the many thousands of activists up and down the country.[19]

This meant that the audience was encouraged to be proactive and empowered to determine its own cultural activity.

An identificatory and loyal relationship was also established, primarily through the company displaying knowledge of particular events and grievances, a localized awareness which was remarkable for a national touring company. This understanding was achieved through intensive research and by drawing on the specific knowledge of the network. For example, venue notes relating to the tour of Scotland with *One Big Blow* contain comments which specifically detail the socio-economic concerns of individual areas in relation to the play's subject matter of mining:

Shotts – At one time there were over twenty pits working in that area – no longer any mining. Very close-knit community. . . .

Gorebridge – Small mining town in East Lothian near Edinburgh. It is understood that local pit is closing, though situation is now confused. NCB accused of allowing miners' houses which they own to fall into disrepair – suggesting that they have been planning to move out of Gorebridge for some time.[20]

This insight facilitated the perception of a sense of caring in the company. Rather than being perceived as just another date on a tour, the diverse constituencies could appreciate their importance to the performance event and the immediacy of it, since the company was able to draw on local knowledge to inform its content and to strengthen the political resonance of its performances. Thus 7:84 (England) succeeded in instilling a sense of pride in and ownership of the company through determined and sustained action which promoted its familiarity with and relevance for a series of localized communities.

This also served to establish a cultural identity that challenged the breakdown between the audience and the performers, the sense of 'us and them' – a division which is paramount to the majority of mainstream theatre, which opts to mythologize the theatrical process and the performer, rendering it and them strange. This was similarly counteracted by after-show discussions which physically and metaphorically transgressed the stage/audience divide.

The company would remain in the performance space as it resumed its non-performative status, with the audience now reinstated as the primary inhabiters of the space. Company members would engage with the audience's comments and responses to the evening's entertainment and inquire how the show related to their experience. Hence a process of 'looping' developed, a correlative relationship which literally and symbolically represented the interdependence of the community and company.

I am not suggesting that the company consistently attracted a staunch working-class audience, or that non-politically active participants were immediately drafted for the 'cause'. What I am arguing is that during the company's existence it did, in many venues, initiate and consolidate a fruitful collaboration with an audience which was not to found in other sectors of cultural activity.

Subsidy – Withdrawal and Response

This is a connection which is difficult to quantify in terms of effect, but it almost certainly led to the company receiving widespread support during its campaign against the Arts Council's decision to cut its revenue funding in 1984 as part of the *Glory of the Garden* initiative. The Arts Council received such a substantial response inquiring about this particular withdrawal of funding that a standard reply had to be drafted by Jean Bullwinkle, the deputy drama director. This asserted that the *Glory of the Garden* list was 'compiled with the greatest of care and on the basis that withdrawal from these specific clients would cause the least damage in national terms to the provision of drama in this country'.[21]

However, there were many prepared to contradict this premise. In a flyer handed out to members of the *Six Men of Dorset* audience, Neil Kinnock stated:

If the Arts Council effectively abandons enterprises like 7:84 it will have abandoned its central purpose. In the process it will encourage the idea that 'culture' is an exotic island that can only be inhabited by the affluent and the elevated.[22]

The Arts Council was sent hundreds of letters containing vigorous protest and requests for reconsideration, in addition to a petition which had approximately ten thousand signatures. These letters were written by a diverse constituency, from individual spectators to Members of Parliament and arts figures such as Joan Littlewood and Arnold Wesker. The majority cited not only the

Addressing the audience in the 7:84 (England) production of John Burrows's play about coal-mining, *One Big Blow*, 1980 (photo: Syndics of Cambridge University Library).

critical acclaim the company had received, but the unusually strong working-class audience composition and the remarkably close relationship the company had established with its audience.

Ironically this unique relationship was also recognized and acknowledged by several Arts Council drama advisors who reviewed 7:84 (England) performances. Thus, Nicholas Barter wrote of a performance of *One Big Blow* at the Half Moon on 13 January 1981, 'Rarely have I seen a company win round its audience as this one did. . . . Few companies have the background of ten years of this kind of work, the strength of cast, and the confidence to "really look the audience in the eye" as this company.'[23] Similarly Patrick Masefield wrote of a performance of *School for Emigrants* at Solihull College of Technology on 27 March 1984:

Where the show is strongest is in its sure understanding of community theatre techniques – the easy dialogue between members of the audience – in the deflation of any threatened theatrical pomposity and in the speed, fluency, and warmth with which a cast of five move from scene to scene. . . . This was one of the most enjoyable evenings I have had in the last year, for warmth of performances and an occasion on which everyone from organizer to cast to audience were talking to each other.[24]

A Climate of Repression

The decision to cut the company, the disregard for the campaign against the cut, and the complete denial of the audience 7:84 (England) generated were indicative of the pervasive influence of the right-wing ideology of the state in Britain in the 1980s. The world from which 7:84 evolved, which had to do with class-consciousness, ideological resistance, and the recognition of a plurality of cultural activity, had virtually disappeared, displaced by the promotion of individualism initiated by Thatcherism, continued under Majorism, and embraced by New Labour.

Throughout the 1980s the state set about eroding the last bastions of class consciousness and disempowering activists. Traditional working-class communities were devastated by the decline in traditional industry, by structural unemployment, and by a sustained campaign to undermine trade union activity. As this reactionary ideology took hold, it obviously had ramifications for a company rooted in the primacy of class-struggle and a faith in the whole notion of class identification and group solidarity – a faith that, as we have seen, uncompromisingly permeated all aspects of company policy and cultural practice. As McGrath admitted: 'So there was I, basing my whole artistic practice on the concept of "class consciousness", and there was the leader of my country telling me it didn't exist.'[25]

For some time cultural theorists had been suggesting a more fluid society where rigid theories of class polarization were obsolete. The homogeneity of the working class was rightly questioned in relation to sexual, racial, and working-status identities.[26] 7:84 (England) had responded to this and was attempting to shift progressively into the 1980s, beyond a conventional class-based analysis, in order to explore new political agendas raised by unemployment, racism, socially constructed gender identity, and the destabilizing of the institutional Labour Movement.

This was evident in such plays as *Sus*, *Trafford Tanzi*, and *School for Emigrants* which were toured during the early 1980s. However, the company still presented working-class solidarity as both desirable and necessary for the benefit of society, inferring that what was required was a recognition of the multiplicity of relations involved and the promotion of a working-class agency which integrated the complex interplay of discourses and sites of contestation which were rooted in more specific relations of social and political subordination.

Unfortunately the developing political climate and resurgence of centralized state intervention were beginning to ensure that any dissenting voices would be severely dealt with. The cutting of the company's funding in the context of mid-1980s Britain suggests an obvious attempt to curtail not just 7:84 (England)'s counter-hegemonic activity, but the potential politicizing and mobilizing force that it offered to its audience. The company's strategies acted as a performative denial of the disregard of collectivism and community ethics, and the popularity of the company served to highlight in theatrical terms the heightening cultural critique of and resistance to the devastating effects of neo-conservative ideology – a critique epitomized in the social protest of the early 1980s and the 1984-85 miners' strike. Just as these pockets of resistance were forcibly dismantled, so was 7:84 (England).

The socio-political context of the mid-1980s heralded a period of severe retrenchment for alternative theatre.[27] Increasingly the Arts Council fulfilled its obligation as an agent of the state, enforcing free-market ethics and acting as a political and cultural policing mechanism. From the mid-1980s the theatre community witnessed the withdrawal of funding from a number of oppositional companies, including CAST, Joint Stock, Monstrous Regiment, and Foco Novo.

Those that remained have been forced to function as business enterprises, competing for resources from sponsors and for revenue funding. This has had far-reaching consequences for the internal organization of companies, as well as dictating a shift in relation to target audiences and subject matter. For example, from 1985 Red Ladder has distanced itself from the radical theatre movement and targeted colleges and youth clubs with young people's theatre.

Political Theatre in the 1990s

In the contemporary context political theatre is isolated and fractured. In the 1970s and early 1980s there was a cohesive countercultural theatre movement which, although diverse, had a sense of common ground and ideological purpose. It could draw on the support of the institutionalized Labour Movement, and associate with wider campaigns of resistance. For many there was a commitment to attracting a new working-class audience; today this would be seen as old-fashioned, idealistic, and harking back to a bygone era when the concept of class had definitive meaning.

The political and cultural landscape has been transformed, political activism is viewed with apathy by the disempowered majority, and aspects of culture are not class but consumer driven. Also, there seems little hope for a radical left-wing theatre practice in the context of the capitulation of the Left. The Labour Movement has faced a radical overhaul, with its leader, Tony Blair, likelier to be found on the board of a media-friendly 'centre of excellence' than supporting an overtly left of centre theatre company.

In contemporary performance practice the primacy of the audience has given way to aesthetic experimentation. The huge growth of physical theatre across Europe has overtaken the popular political theatre movement of the previous generation. This is not to suggest that such companies cannot be political – Volcano's and DV8's physically charged interventions in sexual politics being prime examples. However, their material, in its theatrical and theoretical sophistication, is often culturally elitist, reliant on an informed knowledge of physical vocabulary and theatrical in-jokes.

Similarly the radical interventions made by companies such as Forced Entertainment in exploring dysfunctional urban and political landscapes are often alienating for an uninitiated audience. These companies, and many others, are crucial to the current performance sector, engaging as they do with late twentieth-century society in a dynamic and unconventional way, offering new ways of interpreting social, political, and personal identity – but they remain detached from a wider political framework, and certainly do not attempt directly to politicize, actively engage, and provide a voice for a specific constituency of audience.

Companies rooted in the socially committed tradition of 7:84 (England), such as Banner Theatre, are still in existence, but the work is on a much smaller scale, and is under constant threat since on the whole it does not receive public subsidy. Banner's 1996 show *Criminal Justice* was sponsored by institutions like the Theatre Defence Fund and the Sir Barry Jackson Trust, with some funding given by West Midlands Arts. Banner's work relies on documentary evidence to voice protest, and aims to bring 'Entertainment for a Change' to alternative audiences in venues often organized by local Labour Parties and Trades Councils. However, this type of work is a rarity and widely undervalued.

Clearly, the cultural intervention made by 7:84 (England) to a specific constituency of audience, in terms of its relevance and immediacy at a particular moment in socio-political history, is fundamental to the impact of the company. In the current context it is hard to envisage a time when this could be re-vitalized as an acceptable agenda to be pursued. A new generation of 'Thatcher's children' are developing their own responses to contemporary society, and the cultural impetus faced by companies like 7:84 (England) has been consigned to history.

Notes and References

1. For a history of the alternative theatre movement at this time, see Catherine Itzin, *Stages in the Revolution* (Methuen, 1980), and Sandy Craig, ed., *Dreams and Deconstructions* (Amber Lane Press, 1980). See also Eugene van Erven, *Radical People's Theatre* (Indiana University Press, 1988); Baz Kershaw, *The Politics of Performance* (Routledge, 1992); and Andrew Davies, *Other Theatres* (Macmillan, 1987).

2. This element of choice was fundamental to the accusations of incorporation McGrath levelled at political dramatists such as Howard Barker, Howard Brenton, and David Hare in *A Good Night Out* (Methuen, 1981), p. 14-15. See also John McGrath, 'The Theory and Practice of Political Theatre', *Theatre Quarterly*, IX, No. 35 (1979) p. 43-54.

3. See Baz Kershaw, *The Politics of Performance* (Routledge, 1992).

4. In 1979 a debate was entered into by David Edgar and John McGrath concerning the relative intervention made by alternative theatre practice in working-class communities. See Edgar, 'Ten Years of Political Theatre, 1968-78', *Theatre Quarterly*, VIII, No. 32 (1979), p. 25-33, and McGrath, 'The Theory and Practice of Political Theatre', *Theatre Quarterly*, IX, No. 35 (1979) p. 43-54.

5. See Baz Kershaw, *The Politics of Performance* (Routledge, 1992), p. 132-48.

6. For a discussion of the scale of this circuit see Catherine Itzin, *Stages in the Revolution* (Methuen, 1980), p. xiv.

7. See Steve Gooch, *All Together Now* (Methuen, 1984), and Baz Kershaw, *The Politics of Performance* (Routledge, 1992).

8. Cambridge University Library, 7:84 (England) Theatre Company Archive, Box 8/28.

9. Julie Lockwood, 'A Dramatic Voice for NUM Support', *Sheffield Morning Telegraph*, 30 January 1985, p. 2.

10. Programme Note, 7:84 (England) Archive, Box 8/28.

11. From the programme of *The Garden of England*, which opened on Tuesday 29 January 1985, 7:84 (England) Archive, Box 8/28.

12. See Colin Chambers and Mike Prior, *Playwrights Progress* (Amber Lane Press, 1987), p. 67-75.

13. For a discussion of 'performative contradiction' see Kershaw, 'Poaching in Thatcherland: a Case of Radical Community Theatre', *New Theatre Quarterly*, IX, No. 34 (1993), p. 121-33

14. Letter sent to Arts Council, 16 May 1984, contained within the appeal document, 7:84 (England) Archive, Box 11/28.

15. Mass Observation Ltd., 'Report of the Survey of Small-Scale Drama Groups' Audiences', Arts Council Library, Market Research Collection (1978), p. 9.

16. Ibid.

17. Ibid., p. 17.

18. Appeal document submitted to the Arts Council on 31 May 1984, 'Reasons for Not Terminating the Active Life of 7:84 Theatre Company England', 7:84 (England) Archive, Box 11/28.

19. 7:84 (England) leaflet, 7:84 (England) Archive, Box 8/28.

20. *One Big Blow* Production File, 7:84 (England) Archive, Box 7/28.

21. Arts Council, 7:84 (England) Company Files.

22. 7:84 (England) flyer, 7:84 (England) Archive, Box 8/28.

23. Drama Department Show Report, Arts Council, 7:84 (England) Company Files.

24. Ibid.

25. John McGrath, *The Bone Won't Break* (Methuen, 1990), p. 5.

26. For a detailed discussion, see Paul Gilroy, *There Ain't No Black in the Union Jack* (Hutchinson, 1987).

27. See Baz Kershaw, *The Politics of Performance* (Routledge, 1992).

Gabriel Egan

Myths and Enabling Fictions of 'Origin' in the Editing of Shakespeare

The debate in NTQ about editing Shakespeare has engaged with the practices embodied in recent scholarly projects from the Oxford *Complete Works* (1986) to the continuing 'Shakespearean Originals' series. The issues raised have been philosophical, concerning the nature of authorial subjectivity, and practical, concerning the interventions made by editors in manifestly corrupt or incomplete texts. Here, Gabriel Egan surveys the progress of the debate and responds in detail to Andrew Spong's defence in NTQ 45 of the principles embodied in the 'Shakespearean Originals' series. Rejecting Spong's claim that editorial interference cannot be justified and that early printed texts must be 'cordoned off', Egan argues the necessity of explained interference based on 'enabling fictions' of authorial intention. Since all textual transmission is necessarily mediation, he argues that scrupulous explication of interference is called for, and that this is lacking in the 'Shakespearean Originals' produced to date. Gabriel Egan is completing a PhD on Shakespearean original staging at the Shakespeare Institute in Stratford-on-Avon.

THE CONTINUING debate in *New Theatre Quarterly* about the editing of Shakespeare has reached a stage where a summary of the views previously expressed may be desirable before engaging with the latest contribution by Andrew Spong.[1] Brian Parker began the debate[2] with a criticism of the editorial procedures used by Stanley Wells and Gary Taylor in *William Shakespeare: the Complete Works* (Oxford, 1986). Parker noted that modern technology, in particular cheap photolithography, photocopying machines, and computers, has brought to lone bibliographical scholars an embarrassment of textual riches unknown to their predecessors. The quantity of data available, and the means for processing it, produce a phenomenon familiar to sub-atomic physicists in which the particular means of examining the data have a strong influence on the results. In other words, you get what you look for.

The Oxford edition took as its object of interest the theatrical text as performed in Shakespeare's lifetime, and when editing the extant documents it was this that the editors sought to reconstruct for their readers. Editing towards this ideal led the Oxford editors to certain absurdities, since

an early pre-theatrical draft text would not be given the same weight as a later post-theatrical text: hence *A Midsummer Night's Dream*, to take one of Parker's examples, is dated 1595, but the Folio text, rather than the 1600 Quarto is used as the basis for their version. In a conclusion, the logic of which baffles this reader, Parker called for the return to the practice of conflating early printed texts in an effort to retain the stereoscopic effect whereby multiple early texts with minor differences give the reader a sense of the changes that occur between first authorial draft, final produced version, and, where applicable, later revision.

In a response to Parker's article, the general editor of the Oxford edition, Stanley Wells, began with a collection of small but significant factual errors in Parker's piece.[3] Concerning the substance of Parker's argument, Wells pointed out that editing makes theatricalization necessary since one's copy frequently has things that cannot be staged. The important thing, Wells argued, is how consistently one theatricalizes.

Wells noted that Parker's argument for conflation was in direct contradiction to the 'bricolage' model used by Parker to describe the effect of multiple unstable texts, since, far from promoting an awareness of what has been excluded, the conflated edition prints a composite of a range of texts. Extending this point, Wells argued that once authorial revision is accepted there can really be no responsible conflation since one has no authority for deciding between two different readings if the dramatist first wrote and saw into production the first, and then later decided to remove it and substitute the second.

At this point in the debate a new strand was added by a contribution from Graham Holderness and Bryan Loughrey in which they compared the editorial principles enshrined in their 'Shakespearean Originals' series with those of the editors of the Oxford edition.[4] Holderness and Loughrey claimed that, for all Wells's rejection of the principle, the Oxford edition had used conflation of a particular kind. Although the Oxford editors sought to represent each play as it was first performed, and hence chose for their copy text in each case the earliest theatrical text extant, they also wished to represent the dramatist's habits of expression in preference to those of anyone else.

For this reason the Oxford editors based their accidentals (spelling, punctuation, capitalizing, italicizing, lineation, etc.) on those of another text if that could be shown to represent more faithfully the dramatist's practice. The theatrical text might instead be influenced by a scribe's or a promptholder's habits in these matters. According to Holderness and Loughrey, the modern-spelling version of the *Complete Works* was most guilty of inventing stage directions and conflating accidentals, but they also mocked the process of 'antiquing' in which modern English inventions were turned into authentically archaic early modern English for the original-spelling edition of the book.

For Holderness and Loughrey, the desire to recreate the manuscript upon which an extant printed text was based is just another manifestation of the privileging of handwritten text over printed text, originating in the neo-platonic notion of the 'veil of print'. Since we have only the print version to start from, the underlying manuscript is just an imaginary ideal which we extrapolate from the print version, and hence any attempt simultaneously to 'improve' the print version by reference to the imaginary original produces logical circularity. The policy of the 'Shakespearean Originals', Holderness and Loughrey announced, would thus be to confine conjectures to the apparatus and to reprint the early printed text 'as is'.

Alan Posener began his response to Holderness and Loughrey's piece in much the same way that Wells had begun his response to Parker's, by pointing to a myriad of small errors and misunderstandings.[5] In particular, Holderness and Loughrey's reliance upon a faulty translation of Platter's eye-witness account of a performance of *Julius Caesar*, and their failure to read 'shovel' in *Hamlet* Q1 as meaning 'shovelful', were scorned by Posener. Whereas Holderness and Loughrey emphasized the collective nature of Elizabethan dramatic production, Posener asserted the special role of the individual dramatist. It was, after all, Shakespeare individually, and not the theatrical collective, that Greene denounced as an 'upstart crow' and Meres praised as an English Plautus.

Holderness and Loughrey's detraction from Shakespeare was compared by Posener to the Baconian or Oxfordian position, but rather than desiring a more elitarian 'Shakespeare' they wanted a more egalitarian one. Holderness and Loughrey considered the reference to hypothetical foul papers as an underlying authority for printed texts to be 'idealism', but Posener argued that these hypothetical documents were what Marx would call 'concrete abstractions', which we can meaningfully employ in emendation.

As an example Posener used what appears to be a slip in Holderness and Loughrey's article where the phrase 'substitution . . . for' is used where the intended meaning seems to be 'substitution . . . by', and showed that silent emendation is not only justifiable but also sometimes necessary to the production of meaning. Thus Posener distinguished between two different kinds of interference: emendation needed to restore sense, which the Oxford editors performed, and conflation of different versions of a text, which they did not. Posener did not address Holderness and Loughrey's argument that the Oxford editors engaged in conflation by drawing their accidentals from the text closest to the author's hand, whilst preferring the text closest to first performance as their copy text.

It is to the latest contribution, Andrew Spong's 'Bad Habits, "Bad" Quartos, and the Myth of Origin in the Editing of Shakespeare', that I must respond in detail. Spong attempts to address some of Posener's criticisms of Holderness and Loughrey by using Marxist cultural theory to demonstrate that the positions taken up by contributors to the discussion are exactly those we should expect to obtain amongst editors of these two opposing political persuasions. Spong thus begins by placing the Oxford Shakespeare project and the New Cambridge Shakespeare series in the context of the 'new critical strategies' of the 1980s, and positions them as responses to the loss of dominance suffered by 'orthodox critical beliefs'.

By 'orthodox', Spong here means 'conservative' and he sees a complete victory in the 1980s for interpretation 'from class, gender, sexuality, and race-based perspectives'[6] which others, myself included, might wish instead to represent as an incomplete and ongoing struggle. In reaction to this left-wing success, 'the idealism which formerly had been reserved for the consideration of "Shakespeare's thought" has now retreated to "Shakespeare's text",'[7] and hence the conservative editorial practices of the Oxford and Cambridge editions.

This assertion can be most simply refuted by pointing out that Stanley Wells was hired by Oxford University Press to begin the project in 1977, and Philip Brockbank was hired by Cambridge University Press to commence their series in 1978. Thus these projects began before, and hence not in reaction to, the critical developments which Spong assigns to the 1980s, although he might still wish to argue for change during the gestation of the works if he can find the evidence.

Getting down to 'basics', as Spong, following Posener, puts it, the problem of Holderness and Loughrey's use of Platter's account receives an extraordinary treatment. Posener showed that Holderness and Loughrey had used in their article a rather inexpert translation of Platter's German text which rendered 'streüwine Dachhaus' as the meaningless 'strewn roof-house' rather than the correct 'house with a straw-thatched roof'. Spong uses this as an opportunity to discuss the 'myth of origins' which sends scholars on a wild goose chase 'tracing the origin itself back to *its* source',[8] and derives from an idealistic platonic belief in 'the recuperability of the authorial consciousness'.[9]

Spong plays along with this myth in order to expose it, and hence he admits that 'Holderness and Loughrey draw the quote from E. K. Chambers's *The Elizabethan Stage*'.[10] If this is true, then Holderness and Loughrey ought to have cited Chambers's book, and not Campbell and Quinn's *The Reader's Encyclopedia of Shakespeare* to which they attribute the passage in their article.[11] Spong even toys with the idea of making sense of 'strewn roof-house' by offering 'a reed-strewn Lords' Room at the top of the theatre',[12] for which there is no evidence whatsoever and which a practical consideration of playhouse design rules out.

Having offered this imaginary lords' room, Spong sensibly retracts it and admits that Posener's translation – 'house with a straw (i.e., thatched) roof' – is correct. The error in Holderness and Loughrey's article is particularly important because they repeat it in the 'General Introduction' that prefaces the first three volumes in the 'Shakespearean Originals' series.[13] In subsequent volumes an attempt is made silently to 'improve' Chambers's translation, as we shall see.

Having drawn yet more attention to Holderness and Loughrey's careless use of sources, Spong compounds their error by suggesting that the fault lay not with Chambers but his printers:

It would appear, however, that Chambers's original text features a typographical error, whereby a hyphen has been incorrectly positioned: what should have read 'strewn-roof house' became 'strewn roof-house', and this error has been often reproduced.[14]

Having silently skipped over Campbell and Quinn, to whom Holderness and Loughrey attribute their quotation, and alighted on Chambers, Spong posits something he calls 'Chambers's original text' which contains an error.

One can only wish Spong were more specific. The first printing of *The Elizabethan Stage* in 1923 had the hyphen in between 'roof' and 'house',[15] and all the subsequent reprintings maintained it. The archives of Oxford University Press indicate that in 1944 Chambers made corrections to the text prior to a reprinting, but he left the hyphen in question where it was. It appears that the author did not consider himself or his printers to have made the error that Spong detects.

Perhaps Spong is referring to a hypothetical error in Chambers's typescript from which the first edition was set. If so, this is no more available to us than Shakespeare's foul papers, and Spong's attempted emendation is rather remarkable since it implies that an error in a printed text can be so gross that one may reasonably infer an underlying text and a process of transmission which accounts for it. This is precisely the point that modern bibliographical scholars would attempt to persuade the 'Shakespearean Originals' editors to accept, although I doubt many would share Spong's conviction that his hypothetically misplaced hyphen is a clear-cut case.

Spong's attempt to efface Holderness and Loughrey's slip is unconvincing, but Posener was not entirely fair in writing that 'we can infer . . . that they are not all that good at German'.[16] What Holderness, Loughrey, and Spong appear to be ignorant of is the relatively well-known inadequacy of Chambers's translation of this passage, which led Ernest Schanzer to do the job properly.[17] It is to Schanzer's translation that careful scholars now resort.

Spong did not let Posener's correction rest. In order to prove that the errors which go around come around, he cited Howe's continuation of John Stow's *Annales of England*, in which is described the destruction of 'the play-house or Theater, called the Globe'

by fire in 1613. Spong comments that 'Stow (or perhaps Howe) cannot decide whether to refer to the Globe as "the play-howse" or "Theater".' Note the odd transformation of 'play-house' into 'play-howse' for which Spong, the scourge of those who silently emend, might be held culpable.

But what of Spong's reading of Stow's use of the word 'or' as indicating indecision? Logically, of course, the word is simply being used in its very common sense of 'also known as', as for example one might refer to 'the development of the wireless or radio'. Stow's phrase 'play-house or Theatre' indicates that he knows both terms to be applicable, and many other commentators of the period used the terms interchangeably, as synonyms, within a single sentence.

Spong aims to show that 'the signifier "the Globe Theatre" which Posener refers to is particularly vulnerable' because the recycling of the timbers of the 1576 Theatre to make the 1599 Globe caused Stow's uncertainty. Thus the term 'the Globe Theatre' is radically unstable, Spong argues, because 'Theatre' means both 'playhouse' in general and the particular playhouse which was the '1576 Theatre'. Worse still, Posener risked grave ambiguity by asserting that 'streü-wine Dachhaus' meant 'a house with a straw (i.e., thatched) roof, as was the Globe Theatre', because the Globe was rebuilt after the fire with a tiled roof. Hence 'it is very difficult for the critic to avoid falling foul of the same difficulties that he believes himself to discern in others'.[18]

Spong seems to feel he has given as good as he got, but his argument is based on obfuscation. The builders of the 'Theatre' gave it that name because they knew it to be the classical word for 'playhouse', and the writer of the *Annales* knew this too. Posener's phrase, 'a house with a straw (i.e., thatched) roof, as was the Globe Theatre', is quite unambiguous as a translation of a text securely dated 1599, since there was only ever one Globe in existence at any one time, and in 1599 it had a straw roof.

Spong hopes to have shown us all 'falling foul of the same difficulties' because of our attachment to a 'myth of origins', and to avoid this kind of error he advocates a new approach to textual reproduction:

All that we can do is place a cordon around each version of each text, deliberately keeping the individual Quarto and Folio editions apart rather than attempting to unite them, a principle practically and theoretically instantiated in the 'Shakespearean Originals' series.[19]

If Spong believes this, then his conjectural emendation of Chambers must be rejected as impermissible, since the absence of any underlying texts for the extant print versions of this work must necessitate the placing of a cordon around them. Or perhaps he would 'confine all such editorial speculation to the critical apparatus'[20] of his edition of Chambers, as the editorial policy of the 'Shakespearean Originals' would require. It would be an unreadable edition.

The 'General Introduction' which prefaces each volume of the 'Shakespearean Originals' series has itself undergone silent revision by Holderness and Loughrey. In volumes published since 1995, the wording of Platter's account has been altered so that what was 'strewn roof-house' now reads 'thatched playhouse'.[21] Holderness and Loughrey still attribute their quotation to Campbell and Quinn's *Reader's Encyclopedia of Shakespeare*, which contains no such phrase. Hence the error is enlarged, not reduced, since it now includes misquotation of source. Yet the 'General Introduction' is not separately dated in each volume, and its copyright date is still given as 1992, that of the earlier version.

This 'General Introduction' must qualify as an over-determined collaborative text, its limitations and errors being necessarily symptomatic of the cultural conditions under which it was produced. If they stick to their principles, Holderness and Loughrey cannot correct future impressions without falling into the delusion of 'the recuperability of the authorial consciousness', in this case their own. Once the slip concerning the Platter account was drawn to their intention, intellectual honesty would require that they merely footnote their earlier error.

It is to such absurdities that the fetishizing of particular print manifestations of

text inevitably leads. If the editors were to abandon this fetish they might reasonably revise their 'General Introduction' and give the date of the revision. Their decision to silently alter their source, in effect conflating Chambers's text with their own translation of 'streüwine Dachhaus', is intellectually indefensible.

The 'myth of origin' is indeed a powerful one. It is typified for Spong by the recent statement of the MLA Committee on the Future of the Print Record that 'the future of humanistic study depends on the preservation of original material', since 'new forms cannot fully substitute for the actual physical objects in which those earlier texts were embodied at particular past times'.[22] Spong responds that 'it is frankly difficult to believe that this will always be the case, if indeed it still is', since information technology is rapidly providing new means of reproduction.[23]

Spong has failed to notice that information technology is only one aspect of scientific development, and future scholars are likely to have tools of which we cannot dream for testing the surviving printed versions. As fast as technology produces new means of reproduction it provides fresh reasons why the originals must be preserved. Scholars like Malone felt free to write on the documents they were studying because the only technology available to reproduce them was manual transcription, which would filter out their additions. Had Malone known that his marks would become familiar to scholars the world over, by means of photofacsimile, he undoubtedly would not have made them.

To affirm his mastery of information technology Spong offers three Uniform Resource Locators (URLs) which point to pages on the World Wide Web which have Shakespeare-related content. Within three weeks of publication of his article two of the three URLs were invalid, even when one conjecturally emends 'indxe.html' to 'index.html'. At least one of the URLs, 'http://ves101.uni-muenster', is manifestly incomplete since it lacks a top-level domain which would be either a country code (probably 'de', meaning

'Germany') or an international domain name (for example 'edu', meaning 'education') that takes the place of a country code. Spong may claim that his URLs have been corrupted by the printer, and I would be prepared to accept this explanation, but again the principle of over-determination would stand in the way of correction. One can only assume that Spong, as it was once joked of Derrida, is obliged on principle to make no marks on his proofs.

There is a further problem with his use of printed text to disseminate these URLs. Having commented that it is ironic that the MLA committee's statement about original materials 'was disseminated via electronic mail',[24] Spong displays an equally ironic lack of understanding of the Internet, and especially the World Wide Web. The print medium is not a good place to pass on URLs since it is in the nature of the Web that pages come and go, sites are reorganized and moved, and generally nothing stays the same for very long. A scholarly article, which in the case of *New Theatre Quarterly* might not appear until a year after it is written, is possibly the least appropriate place to disseminate URLs.

In an attack on the squeamishness about 'fiscal matters' shown by Chambers, Spong quotes his comment that the Shakespeare quartos were published by persons 'among whom shifting business relations seem to have existed, and some of whose proceedings, from a literary and probably also from a commercial point of view, were discreditable'.[25] Spong rejects such disdain for sharp practice and asserts that 'a play's use value was equivalent to its exchange value alone, for over and above everything else it was a commodity'.[26]

The danger of this apparently Marxist position is that it comes very close to a right-wing *laissez-faire* notion of use value. Plays are unlike other commodities such as coal and steel in that they embody human self-contemplation. Because they construct dramatic worlds which to some degree mirror and yet simultaneously stand apart from the world we perceive as our own, plays have a use value that exceeds their exchange value.

Such forms of cultural production are the means by which the cultural-ideological superstructure exerts influence upon the economic structure from which it arises. Without this principle of reciprocity, Marxist cultural theory degenerates into a model of mere 'reflection' and 'determination'.

Spong sees the new critical strategies of the 1980s as having 'risen to occupy a position of dominance',[27] but I suggest that at best these strategies are still, to use another of Raymond Williams's terms, 'pre-emergent'. If anything the concern to account for extant texts and edit them with concern both for contemporary dramatic practice and the active intellectual labour of the dramatists shown by the Oxford edition is part of, rather than a reaction to, the shift towards materialism in the 1970s and 1980s.

The 'Shakespearean Originals' series removes the dramatist's ideals from the process and locates a spurious authority in the early printed texts themselves. This is a decidedly un-Marxist rejection of the recoverable active labour of the working dramatist, and amounts to a fetishizing of print. Stanley Wells stood firm against the intention of Oxford University Press to describe their edition as 'definitive' because he holds the conviction that all texts are actively mediated and historically situated, and hence such a label would be misleading. The 'Shakespearean Originals' series is in danger of representing itself as an unmediated reproduction, but its conflation, or ignorance, of press variants belies this self-flattery.

Spong's quotation of irrelevant passages from Marxist texts does not help either the advancement of the particular critical strategies which he supports, or the case for minimal editing of early printed texts. He begins with a quotation from Marx's 'A Contribution to the Critique of Hegel's Philosophy of Right', which he summarizes as 'indignation and denunciation are characteristic of this class of writing [i.e., criticism]'.[28] If the 'Shakespearean Originals' series is criticized for its fetishizing of early printed texts, this is only to be expected since Marx predicted it.

This does not take us very far, but Spong's citations of authority are not really intended to. As with his quotation of the *Annales* and the spurious claim of instability in the referent 'the Globe Theatre', Spong's quotations of Marxist texts throw up a smokescreen to give the impression that Posener's lucid and straightforward objections to Holderness and Loughrey's work were naive.

In the current period of rapid change in means of textual reproduction, there is a pressing need to update Marxist cultural theory, and, were he alive, a scholar such as Raymond Williams would no doubt be engaged upon it. Instead Spong offers a scatter-gun approach of quoting widely from irrelevant sacred scripture (especially the ever-prescient Lenin) as a defence against all charges. Under the guise of deconstructing a 'myth of origin' which, in this context at least, is non-existent, Spong attempts to refute all of Posener's accusations, from a simple, excusable, error of scholarly judgement (using Chambers rather than Schanzer), right through to the wholly unjustifiable shirking of difficult editorial work on early printed texts. The educational and scholarly value of the 'Shakespearean Originals' series of diplomatic reprints of early quartos is diminished by the self-misrepresentation of the project.

Notes

1. Andrew Spong, 'Bad Habits, "Bad" Quartos, and the Myth of Origin in the Editing of Shakespeare', *New Theatre Quarterly*, XII, No. 45 (1996), p. 65-70.

2. Brian Parker, 'Bower of Bliss: Deconflation in the Shakespeare Canon', *New Theatre Quarterly*, VI, No. 24 (1990), p. 357-61.

3. Stanley Wells, 'Theatricalizing Shakespeare's Text', *New Theatre Quarterly*, VII, No. 26 (1991), p. 184-6.

4. Graham Holderness and Bryan Loughrey, 'Text and Stage: Shakespeare, Bibliography, and Performance Studies', *New Theatre Quarterly*, IX, No. 34 (1993), p. 179-91.

5. Alan Posener, ' "Materialism", Dialectics, and Editing Shakespeare', *New Theatre Quarterly*, X, No. 39 (1994), p. 263-6.

6. Spong, p. 65.

7. Spong, p. 66.

8. Spong, p. 67.

9. Spong, p. 66.

10. Spong, p. 67.

11. Holderness and Loughrey, 'Text and Stage: Shakespeare, Bibliography, and Performance Studies', p. 190, note 6.

12. Spong, p. 67.

13. *Hamlet Prince of Denmark*, ed. Graham Holderness and Bryan Loughrey (Hemel Hempstead: Harvester Wheatsheaf, 1992), p. 6; *The Taming of a Shrew*, ed. Graham Holderness and Bryan Loughrey (Hemel Hempstead: Harvester Wheatsheaf, 1992), p. 6; *Henry the fift*, ed. Graham Holderness and Bryan Loughrey (Hemel Hempstead: Harvester Wheatsheaf, 1993), p. 6.

14. Spong, p. 67.

15. E. K. Chambers, *The Elizabethan Stage*, four volumes (Oxford: Clarendon Press, 1923), II, p. 365.

16. Posener, p. 264.

17. Ernest Schanzer, 'Thomas Platter's Observations on the Elizabethan Stage', *Notes and Queries*, New Series, III (1956), p. 465-7.

18. Spong, p. 67-8.

19. Spong, p. 67.

20. Spong, p. 68.

21. For example *Anthonie, and Cleopatra*, ed. John Turner (Hemel Hempstead: Prentice-Hall, 1995), p. 6.

22. MLA Committee on the Future of the Print Record, quoted in Spong, p. 68.

23. Spong, p. 68.

24. Spong, p. 70, note 20.

25. Chambers, quoted in Spong, p. 69.

26. Spong, p. 69.

27. Spong, p. 65, 66.

28. Spong, p. 65.

Cicely Berry, Patsy Rodenburg, Kristin Linklater

Shakespeare, Feminism, and Voice: Responses to Sarah Werner

When I was asked if I would like to reply to Sarah Werner's article in the August issue of NTQ entitled 'Performing Shakespeare: Voice Training and the Feminist Viewpoint', my first reaction was that it was so unfounded in the reality of practical voice work that it was not worth the time needed to respond. But then, re-reading it, I became incensed at the notion that voice teachers, through the work of freeing the voice, are after some romantic notion of connecting with an idyllic past – a notion so utterly absurd that I spoke with my friends and colleagues, Kristin Linklater and Patsy Rodenburg, and we agreed that Ms. Werner's assumptions must be challenged. As Edgar's words imply in the last speech of *King Lear*: 'Speak what we feel, not what we ought to say.' Words hurt, cost, are ugly and violent: but it is my belief that when we reach the point of articulating our dilemmas – it is then that we become free to take action. That is what my work is about. So, to follow are our answers to, and our questions for Ms. Werner.   CICELY BERRY

From Cicely Berry

I SEE MY JOB, as I know do my colleagues Kristin Linklater and Patsy Rodenburg, as intrinsically to do the following: (i) through exercise to open out the voice itself so that the actor finds her/his true potential: after all, do not singers train? (ii) by working on text – hearing and listening – to give the actor choice, and power over that choice.

Now how can you challenge the politics of Shakespeare without these tools, these ways of working? And when I say the 'tools' I mean both the awareness of the physicality of the language, and the breath to carry it out – skills which you can only acquire by working at them.

I would like to reiterate here what I have already said in *The Actor and the Text* – that the exercises which I have evolved over the years in order, as I think, to help the actor connect with the language have come about very often through working with young people – also through extensive work in prisons, both women's and men's establishments, and in closed hospitals.

My main aim has always been to give people the opportunity to speak Shakespeare's language, so rich both physically and in image, and thus perhaps to find some pleasure in being articulate, and in being in touch with their imagination – an experience which I believe can lead them to their own sense of power in words, and thus to their own greater self-awareness.

I have worked on Shakespeare in many countries, many languages: I have worked on *King Lear* in Mandarin, on *Macbeth* in Serbo-Croat – now no longer a recognized language for, due to 'cleansing', it must be either Serbian or Croat, and *that* has big cultural implications. I have worked on *A Midsummer Night's Dream* in Portuguese, in a favella in Rio with the street kids, where police do not go unarmed: all these experiences have been so rich because the plays have touched on political and societal realities so far removed from our own.

Further, we must never forget that the people with the language have the power. The successful politician is the one who can manipulate the language to coincide with the sound of the moment. We want to give actors that power, not to manipulate, but to convey the argument, and above all to challenge the listener.

Now it is up to the actor to use that power in the way he/she wants. Does the writer really think that actors do not ask questions, or that the voice teacher tells them what to do? That is seriously and dangerously to negate and underestimate the integrity of the actor.

Of course my objective is to free the actor's voice – how else can the actor have the power to convey the thought? And that surely must be the prime concern – that we continually challenge and redefine the thought for our own time. So of course that has to be politically motivated. It leaves me wondering what theatre Ms. Werner can possibly have seen.

When I directed *King Lear* at The Other Place some years ago – with some considerable critical success – I took as my central themes two sentences from the play: the first was spoken by Gloucester –'So distribution should undo excess / And each man have enough', and the second by Lear: 'Is there any cause in nature that makes these hard hearts?'

These to my mind are the two central issues of the play: yes, both voiced by men, but the basic enquiry has to do with the societal order of the time and with the relation between male and female in the play. On the second issue, we delved very deeply to discover what we felt was the position of women in Lear's court, and his personal relation to them. I can assure Ms. Werner that there was no 'longing for the innocent carefree days of yesteryear' in our investigation: our imaginations entered a world which was cruel and hard – at times unbearable – akin to our own postmodern culture. I find the inference that the notion that 'freeing the self and the voice distances the actor from any kind of political action' to be outrageously offensive: it is in total opposition to anything I have ever said, taught, or believed in.

It would seem to me profitable for anyone writing a thesis such as that from which Ms. Werner's article derives that they would at some time have direct contact with those they are writing about – and perhaps experience of their teaching in practice. It is so dangerous when academic argument/ language can have supremacy and weight over actual experience. We voice teachers are not talking theories: we are interacting with people and the ways they live. What is theatre for if not to make people more aware?

From Patsy Rodenburg

I HAD TWO major reactions when I read Sarah Werner's article. The first one was of sadness. Didn't she know that the two teachers she was attacking, Cicely Berry and Kristin Linklater, were among the leading forces that had contributed to the political awareness of actors and actresses in the last thirty to forty years? Her point of view can only exist largely because of their work.

Any serious researcher into the history of voice and text work will credit Cicely Berry with releasing not only the actors'/actresses' power, but the political power of the text. Until Cis's work, actors/actresses were repressed and politically manipulated. She has worked all her life to instil into all speakers their personal and political ownership of words and ideas. In America Kristin has done the same, and actors/actresses who have worked with her know this.

My second reaction was a sigh: a sigh of exhaustion. It seems that Werner understands little about actor training and the rehearsal process, and that only undergoing years of work and explanation could fill in the gaps in her knowledge. And do I really have the time to do that?

Questions flow out of me. Has Ms. Werner ever worked extensively on her own voice and taken that work into a text? Has she tried any of the exercises she finds so repressing? Has she worked with experienced actors or directors? Has she ever talked to actors about their work and their knowledge of politics, history, and society? Has she worked alongside a living playwright? Has she ever seen the incredible capacity even inexperienced actors have to interpret a text from different perspectives? The questions go on and on.

One of her complaints is that we don't spend enough time educating actors about history and repression, and about the academic use of language. Doesn't she know that the vast majority of actors all over the world are amazingly well educated and knowledgeable? So much so that it has been historically well documented that actors in repressive regimes – like many of the black actors I recently worked with in South Africa, who had spent years in prison under apartheid and been appallingly tortured – are among the first to be imprisoned, tortured, and murdered precisely because they are politically aware?

Doesn't she know that student actors spend hours of their training learning how to research every aspect of every play? Doesn't she know that directors and actors meet formally or informally many experts on many subjects regarding the context of the play they are rehearsing? Doesn't she know that actresses live with discrimination, and that even to train takes many women along a road of political awareness?

As I write this a female student has entered my office excited that she has found the relevant Norwegian laws that would have repressed Ibsen's women. She is playing Nora in *The Doll's House*. Her passion is partially fuelled by the fact that her parents have disowned her for becoming an actress.

Another preoccupation of Werner is that a free voice is somehow 'wrong' – that somehow teaching the freeing of a voice is a form of manipulation. Does she not realize that without technical vocal freedom a voice, any voice, cannot move and change in any direction, cannot interpret anything with ease?

A free voice opens up many vocal boundaries, though always remembering that any speaker can return to their habits if that's what they desire. A free voice extends the knowledge you have of yourself, but no-one is suggesting you might have to be constant to it. Does Ms. Werner not know that unfree voices are the voices that tire, are ineffectual, and often get damaged.

I always teach through choice, and have never made anyone free their voice – but everyone I have ever taught all over the world, from every conceivable background, likes the feeling of freedom. It's empowering, it's releasing, and, perhaps most importantly, it's fun.

Werner seems to assume that voice and text coaches have enormous power over the final interpretation actors and directors reach. This assumption is simply not true. A good coach offers starting points in the work. All these points can be jettisoned at any stage by actors and directors. If coaches have any power, it is in the teaching of craft, the handing out of tools that can be used by the actor in any way they wish. I also hope I teach a notion of self-discipline in the craft and the right of the artist consciously to make any decision about interpretation that has to include breaking any rule I or anyone else might teach them.

The craft work of voice and text includes exercises that are sufficently repeated so that the actor can 'forget' the work and make any choice with their voice and the word. All work done in rehearsal has to be flexible. Actors are employed to change. The very nature of theatre is about transformation. Actors can and do change their interpretation of a text on an almost daily basis, until ideas and notions are fixed with a director. Even then actors recognize that their work can change when it meets an audience. The final interpretation of a play might be the complete opposite of the one explored within the voice and text work.

Even the shortest period of watching any rehearsal will reveal to observers that actresses are very aware of feminist issues. Many of them have so often had to confront sexism head on that it would be irrelevant and patronizing to suggest they might need to be educated about feminist issues. We all know that it is harder for female students and professional actresses even to get training, let alone to get work, and that even in working they have constantly to experience discrimination.

Having spent many years working alongside great living playwrights, I can assure Werner that no writer would tolerate a voice coach censoring their play. If I find the politics of a play immoral, I have the choice not to work on a play; otherwise my job is to release the play, trying to render the text as clearly as I can – giving actors/actresses a springboard to take off from.

Lastly, Shakespeare – but it is surely unnecessary to defend him. All over the world, in many cultures, environments, prisons, schools, hospitals, theatres, and community centres I have been asked to work on Shakespeare's plays. Why? Initially I thought it was because he is respected academically. No: people want to speak his text. They want to embrace the work because of his humanity towards all people. The truly repressed seem to recognize this better than those who want to pick at him and reduce greatness. Men, women, and children find in his work compassion and peace – the peace of being known and finally respected.

From Kristin Linklater

SARAH WERNER's article highlights the endemic split between academic theatre and professional theatre in general, on the one hand, and academic feminist theatre and the very active women's theatre movement on the other. In the United States the split is exemplified by the experience of the 'Women and Theatre' forum of the Association of Theatre in Higher Education. Initially this forum was peopled by a good mix of professionals and academics interested in women's theatre. They came so consistently to blows (verbal blows, but ugly), that eventually the professionals pulled out, leaving the verbiage to the academics.

It is well known, though not widely acknowledged among the protagonists, that the feminist cause within American theatre is riven and fragmented by the splintering of gay women from straight, non-white women from white, socially active women from politically active women, and academic theatre women from professional theatre women. It is not surprising to find Sarah Werner tortuously fashioning a PhD thesis based on an attack on three women prominent in the professional theatre training world.

I suppose I should let the attack slide inorder not to add to the general disarray in the women's theatre field, which in turn reflects out into the larger world and contributes to the difficulty women have in developing a unified political agenda. But Ms. Werner's sweeping assumptions and cavalier characterization of my work and the work of Cicely Berry and Patsy Rodenburg as reactionary, anti-feminist, and somewhat stupid are irritating. I am needled into making a wild swing back at her.

Ms. Werner interprets the idea of vocal freedom and a natural voice from the judgement seat of feminist historicism. She correlates voice work that restores the speaker to a deeper, more direct and instinctive connection with the self (the words she uses in clearly derogatory senses are 'primitive', 'innocent', and 'healthy') with nostalgic longing for innocent, carefree days of yesteryear'. She accuses Berry, Rodenburg, and me of trusting Shakespeare to such an idolatrous degree that we romanticize the past and deny that there were some less than charming aspects of Elizabethan life. We have failed to 'problematize' history.

My simple, primitive response to this is to ask Ms. Werner to stick to history and let me focus on voice work, but I can't help wondering what kind of innocence leads her to assert that 'Language that is organic and natural is not language that challenges societal structures.' If she would problematize today's repressions and let a deep breath into her body she might find herself, as I find myself, on the exhilarating front lines of a daily struggle with the rigid linguistics of an embattled patriarchy.

I just want to touch on a couple more of the points upon which Ms. Werner attempts to build her argument. Does she really think that Cicely Berry, Patsy Rodenburg, and I believe 'that the characters are real people' and ignore 'the fact that these are fictional characters created by the dramatist'? My distinguished colleagues certainly are aware that plays are written by playwrights. I apparently shocked Ms. Werner by anachronistically ascribing an inner child to *King Lear*. Had I written *Freeing Shakespeare's Voice* for an academic readership, the lighthearted liberties I take with psychology and dramaturgy, designed to enliven the actor's imagination, would have been replaced with humourless, well-documented, and copious footnotes. Because it's not that sort of book, it becomes a perfect target for the slings and arrows of Sarah Werner's PhD. But it is a practical, popular, actor-friendly textbook, as are the books of Berry and Rodenburg.

Next: while I admit to an anti-academic bias in my work, I refuse to allow the academy to hold a monopoly on the intellect. The point I make over and over again both in *Freeing the Natural Voice* and *Freeing Shakespeare's Voice* is that the actor needs to restore the balance between intellect and emotion that has been conditioned out of us both by the evolution from an oral culture to a print and technological culture over the last five hundred years, and by the mind/body split inherent in western educational strategies.

Ms. Werner suggests that any attention paid to the emotions or the psyche obliterates the intelligence. In this she supports the aforesaid western educational strategies and proves herself a true grandchild of Descartes. Even the body and the breath are suspect in her pursuit of pure feminist performance.

I am bemused by the implications of the final statement in Werner's article: 'But until actors can escape the need to be organic and true, voice training will continue to place stumbling blocks in the way of feminist performances.' Does this mean that, to be politically correct, feminist performances have to be inorganic and untrue? Who are the audiences for these performances? Feminists who have transcended the need for breath or body, who never laugh or cry in public and dwell in a de-oxygenated cerebral utopia with a language all its own?

Finally, I cannot fathom Ms. Werner's mission to pit the freeing effects of voice work against the tide of feminism, but I do understand why she leaps to the conclusion that I am an arch-conservative because I have an opinion about the universality of the classics and because I believe that Edward de Vere, the 17th Earl of Oxford, wrote the plays attributed to William Shakespeare. Attributing genius to a member of the aristocracy is bound to open one to accusations of extreme right-wingery and to arouse vitriolic rage in entrenched Stratfordians. I am inured to that: I would like, however, to maintain the right to define my own personal politics which, looking at the world on a daily basis, appear to me as several leagues left of centre. Indeed, a newspaper interview with me this summer defined part of my 'life's mission' to be 'toppling patriarchal oppression'.

This summer I played King Lear in my Company of Women's all-female production of the play. Cicely Berry refers to her production of *King Lear*, and to the political themes that inspired it. Our production was centred in Cordelia's choice to say nothing in a patriarchal world which had made a commodity of love, and where truth-telling was rewarded with banishment. 'Speak what we feel, not what we ought to say' was the lesson we sought to underline.

In addition to our mission to present Shakespeare's plays performed, informed, and transformed by all-women casts, we offer workshops that help strengthen and support the power of women's and girls' voices. Why? Because we believe that theatre is an ideal vehicle for social change, and that freeing the voices of women and girls creates powerful agents for that change.

When the Company of Women is attacked for not fulfilling the political agenda of one or another of the various splinter groups of the women's theatre movement, we resort to a feeble attempt at humour. We say we are non-phallophobic philogynists: multi-cultural, multi-generational, multi-sexual – heterosexual, bisexual, gay, celibate, and past it. It's true, it's not very correct, but it gets a laugh once people figure out the word-play. Our voices are huge.

I am sorry that I may not, according to Sarah Werner's criteria, claim the name of feminist. I will go on doing what I do, however, knowing that a voice that is free will always be used to challenge the status quo because it resonates from a conscious and individual intelligence that cannot be brainwashed by education, culture, or politics.

Tony Howard

Behind the Arras, through the Wall: Wajda's 'Hamlet' in Krakow, 1989

The list of female Hamlets, in which the most familiar names range from Siddons and Bernhardt to Frances de la Tour, is extraordinarily long. Tony Howard here discusses a great but much less familiar production featuring a female Hamlet, both in its socio-political context and in the context of the earlier work of its director, Andrzej Wajda. Teresa Budzisz-Krzyzanowska was Wajda's Hamlet in *Hamlet (IV)* – which, momentously, opened in Poland in 1989, just as the Solidarity-led opposition came to power. Tony Howard, who is writing a cultural history of the phenomenon of female Hamlets, teaches at Warwick University. He has written for NTQ on Polish subjects ranging from the Marxist work of Jozef Szajna to such oppositional groups as Theatre of the Eighth Day and

THEATRICAL THEORY must be grounded in theatre practice. Some productions make the connection explicit.

Since the late nineteenth century, but especially since 1945, East European Shakespeare has forced us to read the plays – and the fact that they refuse to disappear – politically. Productions throughout the Cold War period, and in the more chaotic climate that has replaced it, have reminded us of the urgent connection between public performance and ideology which new historicists and cultural materialists have explored in the academy and via (polemical) scholarship but which has always really been a matter of current, lived reality.

When Essex attempts a coup or Ceaucescu dies, connections become obvious; but they are always there. And of course 'political' is a word with fluid meanings: Angela Carter's carnivalesque feminism in her Shakespearean novel *Wise Children* is political, too, as was the loathing of most London reviewers confronted with Peter Sellars's *Merchant of Venice* when it visited the UK. They declared war on the barbarians – Hispanics, Asians, Jews, Blacks, homosexuals, and intellectuals, and all Americans to a wo/man. Of course we too often ignore the process of cultural production close to home, and we over-simplify it in other countries. For example. . . .

The election of the first Solidarity government in 1989 made Poland the eye of the storm that demolished the post-war 'settlement' and replaced the old tensions with new ones. How neat it seemed when one heard – that very summer – that Andrzej Wajda, whose films had symbolized Solidarity for the world a decade earlier, was producing *Hamlet* with an actress in the title role. Was this triumphalism, with Margaret Thatcher as the Prince? In the event, no: to see it was to experience an education in the subtlety with which art can reflect ideology.

Some Part of Poland

What kind of evil is presented by King Claudius? . . . What is the need of this play in our present time? . . . Is it a play which will drug the audience, make it indifferent to the events of contemporary life with all its conflicts, or will it arouse in the audience a protest against negative powers?
(Michael Chekhov, 1942)

It's a commonplace but it is true that before the publication of Kott's *Shakespeare our Contemporary* the dominant assumption in the British theatre from the Restoration to the age of Gielgud and Olivier was that 'Shakespeare' was timeless and uniquely uncommitted – the 'comprehensive soul' whose works were gifts for great actors, inspirational individualists whose sacramental task was to bring poetry and psychological insights to life.

Kott's proposal – immediately seized on by Peter Brook and Peter Hall in their short 'engaged' phase – was that the plays' value did not lie in the (nationalist?) myth that they restored contact with the glories of the sixteenth and seventeenth centuries, but in their ability to comment on the traumas of the twentieth: 'What matters is that through Shakespeare's text we ought to get at our modern experience, anxiety, and sensibility.'

'Shakespeare our contemporary' meant Shakespeare as collective self-examination. Kott's insistence on the cruelty of the *Dream* or the pessimism of *The Tempest* drove many British academics to accuse him of journalistic vulgarity. But in his own post-war Poland the grim contemporaneity of Shakespeare's stories was not only self-evident, it was a cultural lifeline. In a society where writers were censored and metaphorically (or literally) caged, classical drama offered scope for public coded commentary on the nation's life. Through the 1950s *Measure for Measure*, *Richard III*, and *Macbeth* – studies of the emergence of state repression – were used to confront East and Central Europe's cyclic problems of autocracy and terror. And so, of course, was *Hamlet*.

From 1956 to 1968

In February 1956 Krushchev denounced the crimes of Stalin. This historic but carefully limited liberalizing gesture coincided with an explosion of creative energy in Polish theatre. That year the Stary Theatre, Krakow, presented Leszek Herdegen in a *Hamlet* (designed by Tadeusz Kantor) which inspired Kott's essay 'Hamlet after the Twentieth Congress', later one of the key chapters of his book.

Here, Hamlet became the modern intellectual, brooding on political and existential freedom in a world controlled by meaningless self-perpetuating power structures. Kott welcomed the Stary *Hamlet* for its 'terrifying clarity': 'This interpretation was so suggestive that when I reached for the text after

the performance, I saw in it only a drama of political crime. . . . Hamlet is mad, because politics is itself madness, when it destroys all feeling and affection.'

In a totalitarian context, the fact that Hamlet overthrows tyranny but dies as he strikes makes the brief flash of hope which the play offers at once inspirational and disturbing. The concepts of freedom and tragic determinism rule each other out. And theatrical paradoxes mirrored political ones: Krushchev proclaimed the thaw and crushed the Hungarian uprising in the same year. After Hitler and Stalin, it was inevitable that the Polish theatre should show Claudius's regime as a too-familiar militarist bureaucracy, and that Fortinbras would become an appallingly ambiguous liberator.

Poland's three great quasi-absurdist dramatists all reworked the Hamlet motif in their most influential plays. Tadeusz Rozewicz's *The Card-Index* (1960) focuses on a bedridden Everyman-Hamlet bound and confused by the post-war welter of loyalties, doubts, and debts. In both Witold Gombrowicz's *Marriage* (1953) and Slawomir Mrozek's *Tango* (1964) the new Hamlet overthrows his parents but graduates into despotism. Gombrowicz makes him a soldier returning home in 1945, while Mrozek creates a sullen student who never leaves home at all.

In both cases Freudian fantasies become Stalinist nightmares: Gombrowicz's new Hamlet mutates into Richard III, while Mrozek's intellectual ends up dancing the tango in the arms of a homicidal thug. Fortinbras – who sacrifices thousands to seize 'some part of Poland' and annexes Denmark without a shot (there were echoes of the Russians' refusal to help the Warsaw Rising) – became a real problem, from Zbigniew Herbert's poem 'Elegy of Fortinbras' to Janusz Glowacki's 1980s black comedy *Fortinbras Got Drunk*, where the Ghost is a trick arranged by Norwegian secret agents to destabilize Denmark.

Yet Mrozek's scepticism about youthful idealism proved too harsh. Poland's next great political and cultural upheaval came in 1968, the year of international student protests and the crushing of the Prague Spring.

The intimate relationship between politics and Polish art was never clearer than when Warsaw students took to the streets to condemn the banning of the nineteenth-century anti-Russian classic *Dziady*. Later that year in Lublin, close to the Russian border, Kazimierz Braun packed Elsinore with young people in sweaters and jeans and made Hamlet a political prisoner.

'Hamlet' and the Polish Tradition

There was a national theatrical tradition behind all this. The first Polish professional *Hamlet* was staged in 1797, two years after the forced abdication of the last Polish king and the liquidation of the Polish state. The director and leading actor, Wojciech Bogus-lawski, had been heavily involved in the Kosciuszko Insurrection whose defeat led to the division of Poland between Russia and the Austro-Hungarian Empire and – since despotism must work culturally as well as through violence – to the suppression of the Polish language. Boguslawski became known as the father of Polish theatre. Later the leading Romantic poets, including Adam Mickiewicz (*Dziady*) and Juliusz Slowacki, wrote visionary dramatic epics in exile which established the belief that if all else failed Polish drama must be the last refuge for national passion and the dream of justice.

Polish theatre is extraordinarily self-referential. Polish writers and directors have always packed their work with intertextual allusions, reworkings, and parodies in a continuing moral debate with the national repertoire, because the intelligentsia had assumed for themselves the key role of inventing and refining myths for a country which did not exist. At the heart of the myth stood Mickiewicz's Konrad, the hero of *Dziady*, a tormented Byronic martyr – lover, poet, political prisoner of the Czar.

In a *fin de siècle* game with fact and fiction, the symbolist writer, director, and painter Stanislaw Wyspianski resurrected Konrad in *Deliverance* (1903), but made him an impotent fantasist as well as Mickiewicz's artist-revolutionary. Whereas *Dziady* swept the audience and Konrad panoramically across Eastern Europe, from Warsaw and Lithuania to the Siberian prison camps, *Deliverance* locks them inside a theatre, that palace of dreams and lies – specifically in the Juliusz Slowacki Theatre, Krakow, where the first performance actually took place.

Whereas Mickiewicz's Konrad was a poet-rebel-martyr, tormented by Satan and saved for his mission by priests and angels, Wyspianski made him an actor. His is a complex play which deconstructs its own patriotism and idealism and diagnoses a false streak of self-indulgent histrionics close to the nation's heart. Wyspianski anticipated Pirandello's experiments with madness, illusion, power, and the kaleidoscopic nature of theatre itself.

Konrad has been called the Polish Hamlet: Wyspianski developed the analogue. In *Deliverance* his Konrad quotes Shakespeare on theatre's power to catch the conscience, to be a court where the nation judges itself. But at the same time, and also like Hamlet, he attacks those who mask their impotence with puerile gestures: 'Poetry away, thou art a tyrant!'

A year later Wyspianski wrote a long study of *Hamlet*, presenting it as a play so relevant to Poland that it should be staged in the corridors, crypts, and chambers of Wawel, the royal castle in Krakow where many of Poland's leaders lay entombed. This became a key text for twentieth-century Polish theatre because it demonstrated how classical culture could be made local and 'contemporary' and it established the idea of the *environmental* production, where the history of an unconventional performance space could become part of the meaning of the event.

When the film director Andrzej Wajda directed Shakespeare's tragedy in Gdansk in 1960 it was widely assumed that his Hamlet would be Zbigniew Cybulski ('the Polish James Dean'), who played the alienated anti-hero of Wajda's *Ashes and Diamonds*, to ram home the play's modernity. Instead he cast the more classical Edmund Fetting and based much of his interpretation on Wyspianski's study, convinced that this allusion would connote contemporaneity, but at a distance.

He followed Wyspianski's stress on 'the evolution of events' rather than character, and though there was a conventional proscenium stage, elegant scaffolding broke the space up into compartments which evoked Wyspianski's fusion of Elsinore and Wawel. Characters drew curtains to hide in solipsistic boxes, but the action could become simultaneous, with all society on display. 'Denmark's a prison': what sort of building was Poland?

Wajda and Hamlet

In the 1970s a secret memorandum of the Department of Ideological and Educational Action of the Central Committee of the United Polish Workers' Party declared that Andrzej Wajda 'is not politically involved in a pro-Marxist sense': worse, he dared to imagine himself an '"objective judge" of both the past and the present – it being his opinion that he has the right and the possibilities to apply the standards of humanism and morality to the problems of the world without having to resort to Marxism'.

Wajda's first films had been, at least outwardly, enthusiastically pro-Communist, but he was increasingly at odds with the censors: 'The real problem', he wrote, 'is how to conceive of a work that will render them inoperative.' This was one reason why he was drawn to classical theatre. Another was the chance to explore complexity:

I never touch those texts; I don't try to 'improve' the scenes; I do not change a word of dialogue; I never adapt. For weeks on end I read and reread the text with the actors, firmly believing I will find an answer. This process makes me a better director, more attentive and more ambitious. . . . These analytical rehearsals, carried out in peaceful surroundings, give us a better chance of understanding the mysteries of *Hamlet*.

But perhaps the most important motive was that the theatre

taught me to tell the difference between what is natural and what is true. Theatre is the art of form. The imitation of life, which is essential for the cinema, does not suit its purposes. Theatre takes place both on the stage and in the auditorium; the two indispensible elements are the actors and the audience.

In 1980 Solidarnosc suddenly seemed to make the theatre of symbols and allusions redundant. Polish writers dared to examine recent history openly while the documentary genre regained credibility. Wajda's *Man of Iron*, with Jerzy Radziwilowicz as a dissident Gdansk shipyard worker, fused fiction with *cine vérité* – Lech Walesa himself appearing as a guest at the hero and heroine's wedding – and Wajda became so involved in the shipyard's politics that he organized the ceremonies when a monument was erected to victims of state violence.

But Wajda chose this moment to stage two new versions of *Hamlet* for the Stary Theatre. First the company performed a programme of 'Scenes and Soliloquies' at Wawel itself, to honour Wyspianski's vision of *Hamlet* as a play for a free Poland, then the same cast opened a full version in the Stary Theatre on 28 November 1981. Two weeks later the regime struck. Martial Law was imposed, Solidarnosc was banned, activists were imprisoned, and the country sank into bitter and enforced inaction. *Hamlet* reopened in March 1982: Fortinbras and his soldiers patrolled the stage, eyeing the audience coldly like General Jaruzelski's militia.

Two years later the Stary staged Wajda's *Antigone*, taking the concept of the 'contemporary classic' further than ever with a modern-dress allegory of Polish history since 1944. Sophocles' Chorus shifted its identity to reflect the growing alienation between the Party and the people: first it appeared as returning partisans, then as party bureaucrats, student protesters, and finally the shipyard strikers of Gdansk.

Did Martial Law prevent Soviet intervention and thereby prepare the way for Gorbachev? Certainly it could not hold back change. In June 1989, as the Soviet system began to collapse at its heart, Poland held democratic elections which produced a Solidarnosc-led government under Tadeusz Mazowiecki. On 29 July Wajda – a senator in the new administration – opened yet another *Hamlet* at the Stary, closing the Jaruzelski era as his 1981 version had unwittingly begun it. This was *Hamlet (IV)*

Of course the end of the post-war world order was not the end of history, but in Europe it did end the ideological bipolar division of reality into twin ('free' and 'evil') systems. Amidst such convulsions, no astute director could still offer Hamlet as simply the suppressed voice of liberation, nor could the 'other' – Claudius's Elsinore – remain a crude police state. Now the 'New Europe' demanded a reimagined *Hamlet*, and Wajda, following Wyspianski again – *Deliverance* this time – set it in a theatre. Moreover, instead of making Hamlet a Polish hero, this was a postmodern production with complex and *international* roots, dismantling certainties. It was an enquiry into commitment, but into identity too.

Wajda has said that the key to film-making (and we should apply it also to innovative theatre) is *'the idea'*: the director must provide an image or new perspective that ensures that 'the general becomes specific, the abstract concrete, and the idea incarnate as human drama.' *Hamlet (IV)* was unusually rich in simple, forthright, and brilliant 'ideas'. The title itself was multi-referential: it evoked Pirandello (*Enrico IV*); it drew attention to Wajda's own attempts over thirty years to do *Hamlet* justice (and acknowledged his relative failure); and it suggested the idea of theatrical succession and continuity.

The Dying Conscience: Vladimir Vysotsky

As we shall see, *Hamlet (IV)* must be appreciated as a collective creation, but it stemmed from Wajda's personal responses to the work of four outstanding artists – a Russian balladeer, an emigré poet in Harvard, a Japanese female impersonator, and a Polish actress – all brought into collision through an English Renaissance text. As the Cold War world died of exhaustion, the Stary Theatre offered glimpses of a new post-nationalist Shakespeare, intensely local yet cosmopolitan, which scrutinized the phenomenona of theatre and the creative process.

The Russian singer and poet Vysotsky played Hamlet for the Moscow Taganka Theatre in the 1970s. During the stagnant Brezhnev years Vysotsky gave discontented Russian youth a voice until news of his shocking premature death filled the streets. To quote his director, Yuri Lyubimov, in a 'hard epoch' Vysotsky 'managed to sing freely' to an audience of millions: 'Moscow buried him like a national hero.'

Reviewing an evening of Vysotsky's poems and songs in Warsaw in 1989, the critic Elzbieta Baniewicz revelled in the growing freedom of speech and claimed that Poles admired Vysotsky for his sensitivity to

> the savage traits in his fellow-citizens and the stupefying effect of propaganda. Significantly, he was an artist brave enough to speak – some years before the perestroika – about the great tragedy of his nation, about the camps at Magadan and Kolyma where man touched 'the lower depths of fate'. He did so even though he knew that these works were condemned to public non-existence.
>
> *Le Théâtre en Pologne/Theatre in Poland,*
> September 1989, p. 6

But Wajda's response to Vysotsky was not propagandistic, it was personal and physical. In the winter of 1980 the Taganka visited Warsaw. Wajda:

> I saw Vysotsky play Hamlet for the last time in his life. . . . He was dying from the effort. I hugged him after the performance and cold, deathly sweat was pouring off him. He died a few weeks later.

For Wajda, Vysotsky's death at that moment gave the play and especially the 'To be or not to be' soliloquy new meanings: it meant 'to last to the end, to bear the part's pressure. To play it to the end. To survive.' Wajda became fascinated by the courage and self-exposure involved in playing Hamlet – 'coming out onto the stage, coming out to the audience' – and this became both an intense metaphor for personal commitment and a great act of endurance in itself: *Hamlet (IV)* would be about the high cost of integrity both within and outside the theatre's walls. Vysotsky, Wajda said, 'was struggling not only with his role, but first and foremost with his own suffering.'

Words? Silence? Exile? – Stanislaw Baranczak

Wajda planned *Hamlet (IV)* as a collective laboratory experiment: 'I have never seen a *Hamlet* that worked completely', he wrote. 'Why? Because art is about limitation, elimination, choice, and *Hamlet* is a picture of life itself. I can't direct it, just as I can't direct my own fate. I can only confront it.'

Since the early 1970s he had worked on a thrilling series of Dostoevsky adaptations at the Stary. The first, *The Devils*, was an elaborate example of director's theatre which featured ear-splitting sound effects and masked black figures – demonic stage-hands and executioners – derived from Bunraku theatre; but the later productions stripped the novels down to a series of intense encounters between key characters.

His version of *The Idiot*, *Nastasja Filipovna*, had a cast of two men – Prince Mishkin and Rogozin – who acted out a long, tormented confrontation while the corpse of Nastasja, whom both had loved and destroyed, lay undiscovered. *Nastasja Filipovna* was an event in 'real time': performances always began in private before the audience were admitted, and the actors, Jerzy Radziwilowicz and Jan Nowicki, were completely free to improvise round Dostoevsky's text. Wajda tried to *synthesize* the spirit of the novel through one climactic incident and the influence of Grotowski's 'poor theatre' was palpable in this confessional, overheard piece. Wajda wished to re-examine *Hamlet* using similar minimalistic techniques of focus and elimination: how much text was necessary?

He contacted the emigré poet Stanislaw Baranczak to translate. Baranczak had been involved in the 1968 student protests, and he helped to organize support for industrial workers who clashed with the government in the mid 'seventies. His poetry exposed the distortion of language itself under totalitarianism and his work as an activist foreshadowed Solidarnosc because the Polish opposition had repeatedly been crippled by the mutual distrust of workers and intellectuals.

After Martial Law, Baranczak emigrated and taught at Harvard. Originally, Wajda asked him to translate only fragments of *Hamlet*, five soliloquies, so that in the most private moments Hamlet would speak with Baranczak's modern voice. Every other character would use an antiquated nineteenth-century translation that seemed as false as the official discourse of the state seemed when quoted and deconstructed in Baranczak's own poetry. This experiment in levels of linguistic definition built on the fact that Jerzy Stuhr, Wajda's 1981 Hamlet, spoke the soliloquies to the audience in fluent Italian when the production visited Rome.

Gradually, though, Baranczak wrote more and more. Wajda told him, 'I'll be juggling the fragments I got from you. I like surprises, difficulties, unexpected things.' And he added that this play seemed to require a collage treatment: '*Hamlet*'s greatness lies in a mystery that's hard to solve. It's an awkward work with huge gaps.' For all its length, he felt some essential scenes were missing, so the only way to stage it was to reconstruct it from its heart: 'Any consistent and uniform concept fits this play, which is life itself, like a saddle fits a cow.'

He told Baranczak, 'The whole thing will only come into being with the actors'. Indeed, the play reasserted itself in rehearsal: the production became less minimalist and monologal and Baranczak translated everything – in fact, he went on, despite grave illness, to translate all Shakespeare's plays. Aptly, for commercial and diplomatic reasons *Hamlet (IV)* was first widely seen in America and joined the festival circuit after one premiere performance in Krakow.

Being and Gender: Tamasaburo Bando

In March 1989, Wajda directed *Nastasja Filipovna* in Tokyo at the Benisan Pit Theatre. He had already directed an Italian cast, but the Japanese production was startlingly new. This time Nastasja appeared as a character and, even more important, the Kabuki actor Tamasaburo Bando doubled the role with the 'idiot' Mishkin. Whereas Polish theatres often see an affinity between their own national character and Dostoevsky's brew of politics, hysteria, introversion, and religion, Wajda's Tokyo production was more an investigation of *difference* – cultural, racial, and sexual.

He had used cross-dressing before: he cast an actress in the comic role of a male theatre manager in Wyspianski's *November Night*, and the climax of *Marriage Blanc* by Tadeusz Rozewicz (Yale 1977) is an act of sexual self-transformation, in which an adolescent girl tries to take control of her identity by shearing off her hair and declaring she is her own brother.

After these tentative experiments with gender Wajda found it instructive to work with an actor trained in the disciplined *onnagata* tradition, and it strengthened his wish to use *Hamlet* to investigate the acting process – 'Hamlet is an actor', he said, 'a human being in disguise' – and it confirmed his key casting decision. To quote Teresa Budzisz-Krzyzanowska:

He was fascinated by Tamasaburo Bando: 'What a phenomenon, how great!' He showed me photographs and said, 'If it's possible for a man to play a woman, why can't a woman play a man?'

Hamlet (IV): Teresa Budzisz-Krzyzanowska

Budzisz-Krzyzanowska was born in 1942. She made her debut in 1964 and was quickly cast as Juliet. She joined the Stary Theatre in 1972 and became one of Poland's leading classical actresses, equally powerful in Chekhov or singing torch-songs by Weill. Wajda told Baranczak, 'I think she's the most gifted actor in Poland.'

Wajda had first proposed that she play Hamlet some years earlier, but her reaction was cool: 'It seemed inappropriate just to show off my skills, just to prove I could do it.' After the Tokyo experiment he wanted her to concentrate on transexuality, to 'play a man', but she was far more interested in the tragedy's content than its protagonist's gender, and in fact never did 'play a man' at all. She responded much more to Wajda's idea that it should be a chamber piece, where the audience could watch her taking on the role of Hamlet – spy on her preparations, see her and the character in the gaps between the scripted scenes, appreciate the

Teresa Budzisz-Krzyzanowska as Hamlet.

ways her personality and Hamlet's tragic condition touched or clashed. Teresa Budzisz-Krzyzanowska became in effect *the subject* of *Hamlet (IV)*.

The production played to a small audience of about a hundred which, instead of taking their seats in the auditorium, were ushered to a dressing-room area behind the stage. Suddenly, they were joined by Budzisz-Krzyzanowska, dressed in her own street clothes. They were about to become the privileged witnesses of a complex and painful process of self-transformation as Hamlet, the isolated conscience personified, became the 'scourge' of the nation, and as an actress in her forties merged with the most famous male role in world drama:

Sometimes I entered across the empty stage, sometimes I came in with the spectators, mingling as if I were one of them. The production's structure allowed for improvisation and generally depended on the psycho-physical condition of the evening, on one's imagination, one's ideas, the pitch of thought. It was simply alive.

She wore a fawn coat. She removed it and revealed the familiar black doublet, white collar, and high black boots of Hamlet, then sat and made herself up, looking in a mirror ringed with bright bulbs. Wajda: 'In front of the dressing-room mirror, the soliloquies are confessions of doubt . . . not just Hamlet's, but the actor's playing the role.'

For Budzisz-Krzyzanowska, 'Changing into Hamlet, the attempt even to fit my body into the role, was a separate *étude* in itself before the performance began.' She covered her head with a black veil – 'It was a sign of mourning and at the same time there was a feminine element in all that.' Then:

A gong announcing the start took me by surprise, emotionally naked, because it was as if I'd crept in privately and surreptitiously, testing whether I could play Hamlet, and suddenly I was caught by the situation. And I had to do it.

For the audience, the traditional spatial relationship with actors was transformed: they were stranded in Hamlet's/the actress's private space of thought and withdrawal where, privileged but uncomfortable, they might glimpse their own faces in Hamlet's mirror.

Budzisz-Krzyzanowska was almost never allowed to rest because the spectators saw Hamlet between Shakespeare's scenes – watching, thinking, feeling, and reacting, but never free to forget the weight of responsibility. It was a rare encounter with the committed actor, caught in the nightly offstage drama for which Shakespeare supplied no guidance, no language. 'In a word, it will all be to do with theatre. . . . The actor is the body through which the lifestream of the dramatic character flows.' Wajda said: 'The gender doesn't matter.' More on that later.

To the right, a wide scene-door opened onto the stage and lights and, beyond them, rows and rows of empty plush seats. On that stage, with their backs to us, Claudius and his court acted out the public scenes in a posturing and two-dimensional style to an audience who had not come. In 1989 this was a powerful metaphor for the exhaustion of the dying Jaruzelski regime; for other times and countries it stood for the falsity of all power politics and the shallowness of official histories that push conscience and sincerity into the wings.

In total contrast to the brutish King (Jerzy Gralek), Budzisz-Krzyzanowska's Hamlet was astonishingly sensitive and responsive. Sometimes she watched Claudius's world, even using the stage manager's video monitor to spy more closely. Sometimes other characters entered her space: then they were forced to play more intimately and reveal their secret selves. The production respected cinematic acting in close-up and mocked stage histrionics. When she was abroad, Claudius invaded the dressing room and tried to smash it in a jealous frenzy.

Wajda privileged Hamlet's consciousness so much that when the audience watched Claudius on the monitor they saw *exactly* what Hamlet saw, as if through his/her eyes. Budzisz-Krzyzanowska:

This approach not only demanded that I act but also that I observe everything and sometimes even direct it, because everyone's behaviour depended on me. I couldn't afford one moment of psychological laziness. It was fantastic but at the same time exhausting – sometimes it slipped out of my hands terrifyingly as though someone else's hands were on the rudder. It was very personal, though I hope it wasn't exhibitionistic.

For many spectators, she found, the unrelenting intensity made the play a psychodrama.

The Actor's Creative Isolation

Hamlet (IV) grew out of decades of work Wajda and the Stary ensemble had undertaken together. It explored the actress's creative isolation in a remorseless way, yet its importance for Budzisz-Krzyzanowska herself lay in its exploration of the theatre *as a community*. Shakespeare's Hamlet is revitalized when the Players arrive – they are trusted friends with whom he shares a culture, restoring his contact with the world and providing the tools to test it – but because theatre had been the symbolic mouthpiece for Polish identity for so long, this gained a special political point. The Players who visited Wajda's Elsinore in 1989 showed through their warmth and frankness how authentic communities can survive to protect their values within a false society.

Claudius's court wore heavy Renaissance costumes, but the Players were in modern dress. Their leader (Jan Peszek) was a balding cerebral man with a carpetbag – and a fawn coat like Budzisz-Krzyzanowska's. With their arrival the sense of metatheatre sharpened. The First Player was presented as a great actor and (unlike Shakespeare's)

Teresa Budzisz-Krzyzanowska at the dressing-room table and mirror – 'one of the key images of the production'.

a master of cinematic understatement. The 'Hecuba' speech was close to his heart; he and Hamlet – both observers, after all – knew each other intimately, and he teasingly downplayed his admiration for the Prince's acting till they fell laughing into each other's arms. The scene was touching, but when the Player took the speech over he whispered its harrowing climax into Hamlet's ear.

Peszek was the only person to play two important roles, for he was also the Grave-digger, and this doubling was important. Like the Players' expulsion from the city, it alluded to Martial Law and the leading actors' very public boycott of the controlled mass media. Budzisz-Krzyzanowska:

The fact that the First Player later becomes a gravedigger, just as Krzysztof Kolberger became a waiter and others taxi drivers, had a special meaning at that specific moment. We tried not to make these contemporary allusions too blatant, personally I dislike that sort of artistic oppor-tunism, but it seemed necessary then.

This was not the first Polish *Hamlet* to refer to the actors' boycott and the artists' role in Solidarnosc. In Janusz Warminski's 1983 version at the Warsaw Ateneum, Denmark was a paranoid modern dictatorship and the Players were dignified figures in mourning clothes led by Jan Swiderski, one of Poland's greatest post-war stars. The key difference between this and *Hamlet (IV)* was that at the end of the 1980s pure protest was redun-dant; the Stary could show Claudius's sys-tem collapsing under the strain of its own charades whilst Hamlet fought to feel, think, and speak truthfully – to rehearse for action.

While this reflected the exhaustion of state communism and the sense of imminent change, it was also a celebration of art – the collaborative, immediate art which is theatre – and an investigation into the mysteries of role-play. *Hamlet (IV)* drew on the audi-ence's bitter memories as part of the exploration of authenticity and conscience, the web of allusions. Public falsity was a given, so this production exposed an uncertain inner struggle for personal truth. The production was postmodern but morally active, post-communist before the fact but searching for a new politics.

Like Wyspianski's Wawel *Hamlet*, this was environmental Shakespeare: the key images were the dressing-room table and mirror, the video screen, and the Stary's own architecture. The empty auditorium echoed; the rear entrance to the stage became a no-man's-land between truth and lies (the designer Krzystyna Zachwatowicz walled it with mirrors); and a real black-painted window opened onto the street. Space was fragmented into a set of disconnected visual frames. Budzisz-Krzyzanowska opened the window during the performance:

You could hear the noise of the traffic, singing, drunks, arguments, people's footsteps. It was impossible to fabricate the illusion that something separate was happening in here, it had to correspond to the reality outside. Of course I could close the window if it became too obtrusive, and I tried to enter my own world, to cut off, but it was a clear sign that everything was happening here and now.

Echoes, Allusions – and Gender

If the Stary, like Wawel Castle, was a monument that had survived world wars and a long parade of aggressive ideologies, it was also a workplace, with a unique tradition of classical and modern productions by one of Europe's finest ensembles. *Hamlet (IV)* resonated with artistic allusions as well as political ones, memories of collective achievements. 'The whole production', said Budzisz-Krzyzanowska, 'came into being out of love for theatre and for actors. There were moments we invented ourselves that were only possible in this company, where we'd performed together for decades.'

The Polish audience were aware of the actor as well as the role, so that, for instance, Krzysztof Globisz was not only Hamlet's ally Horatio but also the actress's real-life 'young, talented' friend – supportive (he was the assistant director) and 'eager to help an older female colleague', as she modestly described herself, 'playing a role I can't really carry. Here he comes to help me, with a great deal of tolerance and understanding.' But the production could also joke about the company's internal politics: Hamlet caught Globisz/Horatio reading Budzisz-Krzyzanowska's lines, dreaming of being the Prince.

Despite or because of her gender, Teresa Budzisz-Krzyzanowska was one of the great modern Hamlets – animated yet intensely sensitive, frank, watchful, and astonishingly open. One by one the other characters, compromised, left the public stage and entered her space, and one by one they flinched or looked away as she confronted them and compelled them to gaze into her eyes, which became the mirror of their lives.

She also made Hamlet deeply compassionate and criticized the usual treatment of Rosencrantz and Guildenstern: 'The boys playing Hamlet expose these fellows so unpleasantly, with all their superior knowledge. I've always thought the scene is about true friendship. Hamlet should try everything to preserve this friendship, to protect them from degradation.'

Pirandello-like, she played herself playing Hamlet, but did it with such emotional intensity that the boundaries of acting blurred. Gender was not an issue for most Polish critics. Some – reluctant to discuss the political allegories – complained that Wajda's secular emphasis on roles, the psyche, and state pretence belittled 'the tragic', but Urszula Bielous, for example, praised Budzisz-Krzyzanowska's achievement ('light, effortless' and 'without a shadow of falseness') as her Hamlet sat alone with her love and anguish or displayed 'the pain of self-knowledge before the others' eyes'.

The fact that her gender was not contentious points out differences between East European society and Britain or America in the 1980s. In the USA she discovered that the general assumption was that her motives for playing Hamlet must lie in feminist or gay sexual politics. But because of the role of women's organizations within the Communist system, organized feminism was distrusted in 1980s Poland. For Budzisz-Krzyzanowska,

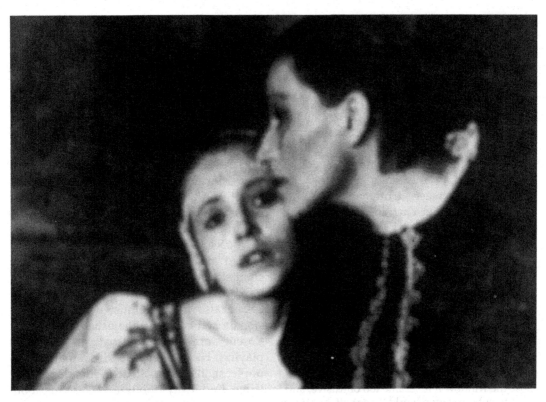

Above: Hamlet, alone with Ophelia. The Polish critic Urszula Bielous praised Teresa Budzisz-Krzyzanowska's 'light, effortless' achievement as, 'without a shadow of falseness', she displayed 'the pain of self-knowledge before the others' eyes'. Below: composite shot of Ophelia juxtaposed with the arrival of the Players.

playing Hamlet was a private exploration of her own life-experience and a response to her own time passing:

I'd played Gertrude in our rather ordinary 1981 production, and I remembered precisely what I didn't like in it. So I kept reading, surreptitiously plotting what would happen if. . . . But I was definitely afraid to think about it seriously. However, there came a moment when I felt, how shall I put it, that I desperately wanted to work on myself – not necessarily in the theatre, it wasn't that I felt unfulfilled professionally – but there came a moment in my adult life when I wanted to stop. I was always running very fast, and as I silently read *Hamlet* it seemed to help me pause.

A Triptych of Women

During rehearsals a complex relationship developed at the heart of the play because of a bond between her, Dorota Segda making her debut as Ophelia, and Ewa Lassek (Gertrude), who was one of the Stary's most respected older actresses but was very ill. Three generations of actresses, three approaches to theatre: 'Ewa Lassek played wonderfully but – it was the intention – in an old-fashioned way, defending her dignity. I took my own route, wild, intractable, and the youngster acted with her eyes wide open, wanting to learn from us both.'

If the overall production set old (the regime) against new (the opposition), the three actresses built a different argument about time and knowledge. At the premiere, the intense recriminations of the Closet Scene became an overwhelming 'fight for life'. 'Ewa acted beautifully but as it were too truthfully. I virtually had to hold her up. She was apologising to me on stage, with tears in her eyes, for being unable to carry on.' Ewa Lassek was only able to play that one fraught performance and died soon after, but her painful contribution echoed the Vysotsky story – and indeed Teresa Budzisz-Krzyzanowska's own commitment. (She herself had to fight physical problems to play the part and says that key scenes, like Ophelia's burial, strained her heart.)

The Queen was recast. The younger Dorota Pomykala took the part on without notice, and, though hers was the Gertrude almost everyone saw, inevitably the three women's joint self-exploration which had been crucial in rehearsal was lost. But even watching *Hamlet (IV)* with Pomykala, it was only in the scenes with Gertrude and Ophelia that one was completely conscious of Budzisz-Kryzanowska as a woman: she seemed to become the conscience of Gertrude and the potential of Ophelia, both of whom were swathed in ornate layers of clothing and seemed somnambulistic and numb.

When Gertrude entered Hamlet's dressing-room after the play (reversing Shakespeare's dynamics) it was the night's first honest confrontation. The distraught Hamlet knelt by Polonius's corpse and Gertrude stroked her child's head, but Budzisz-Kryzanowska forced her to look in her face and share her emotions. Gertrude and the febrile, accusatory figure in black moved in and out of each other's trust.

Though the scene was brief, it reprised key motifs and emotions from earlier moments. Budzisz-Krzyzanowska tried furiously to wake Ophelia and Gertrude to the possibility of a different life, and she painfully reshaped them. Left alone after the Nunnery Scene, doll-like Ophelia ripped apart the book her father had placed in her hands, and in her madness she literally chewed and spat out words. After the Closet Scene Gertrude walked painfully out, supporting herself with a white stick one had never noticed before.

If this subliminal triptych of women contributed greatly to the drama, so did the sense that Budziz-Kryzanowska was cut off – from the other actresses, from most of the men, from the audience, and even from her own face in the mirror:

I tried not to see the audience. The mirror helped me enormously, the very ability to look into your own face as you speak opens amazing possibilities: 'What do I think? What do I do?' So the mirror had multiple meanings. I rarely looked at myself as a woman in it, but this had great significance for me in the scene with the skull and Hamlet's 'Let her paint an inch thick; to this end she shall come.' That was me in the mirror.

Hamlet placed the skull on the dressing-room table as a *memento mori*, having found

Top: the murder of Polonius. Bottom: Budzisz-Krzyzanowska's Hamlet at the makeup table, with Ophelia.

at long last eyes that did not flinch from hers. Often, waiting alone and out of sight at the end of the performance before the applause, she would look at herself in a mirror.

Budzisz-Krzyzanowska's own response to *Hamlet* focused on a 'stark and contemporary' phrase in Baranczak's version of 'To be or not to be', which she paraphrased as: ' "We halt for a moment and lose purpose, and the moment grows into a long, meek life of sufferance." I revolted against this one verse body and soul. Yet often, to make life long, joyful, and beautiful one must do something so ugly that the price may be too great.' She did not try to link her work to the political world through anachronisms and allusions: she underlined consequences.

'Playing for My Life'

Her Hamlet was stunned to realize that her attempt to kill the King destroyed Polonius and Ophelia:

> You commit an act for the good of others – 'cleansing wars to make it better for the next generation', they say, 'so let's slaughter each other now!' It's all futile. The moment Hamlet commits the act – which is horrific to him – he puts himself at risk. Psychologically and philosophically speaking, and in the best of faith, he commits an act against himself.

From the moment of Polonius's murder, her exhausted and appalled Hamlet began to die, fighting to survive to the end as Wajda thought Vysotsky did:

> The emotional explosion over Ophelia's grave brought me to the brink of a heart attack. Hamlet's death isn't caused by a poisoned sword – that's all histrionics, out on the stage – it's a true death, simply from exhaustion, from the terrible effort which living is, which each performance is. One should play every performance as though it were one's last. It's a truly appalling sight when actors take off their make-up in front of the dressing-room mirror. It's like death. And that's how I wanted my Hamlet – playing for my life, in a theatre.

After Ophelia's funeral, Hamlet was desperately weak and could hardly stand – Horatio supported and nursed her tenderly – but must still meet the last challenge. In Wajda's film *Danton* Gerard Depardieu pushes his voice till it becomes hoarse and cracks as Danton shouts for his life at his trial; Budzisz-Krzyzanowska too showed the sheer physical cost of integrity. Life and art plagiarize each other, and the actress recalls the shock when, during the last rehearsals, Mazowiecki took office as democratic Prime Minister and collapsed in front of the television cameras.

In the play, the final duel was fought on the regime's terms – on the main stage. As the duellists advanced and retreated, they moved in and out of the spectators' limited vision. Breathless, half-bewildered, Hamlet somehow sensed that there was something wrong with the pearl. But then Laertes, contemptuous of subtlety, casually stabbed Hamlet in full view. In this version Hamlet's real enemy is time, and finally the body *almost* failed the will. Solidarity: as Hamlet stabbed, Horatio held the King fast. It was Horatio who despatched him.

She stumbled to the seat by the window, the farthest possible point from the blood, and Horatio slid shut the theatre's massive iron fire-door. In the sealed room the sound quality changed so much that their quiet voices almost drowned the sound of Fortinbras's army arriving outside: perhaps death is the only true private moment. Hamlet died, and as Horatio prepared to leave and bear witness with Shakespeare's script in his hand, Fortinbras entered. . . .

Whereas romantic *Hamlet*s typically stopped at Hamlet's death ('Goodnight sweet Prince'), many post-war productions have closed cynically on Fortinbras's amoral triumph. But at the Stary many production strands were tied together in a final *coup de théâtre*. Fortinbras was Jerzy Radziwilowicz, the hero of *Man of Iron*. In his first scene the young general was a ranting, posturing warmonger with plumes in his helmet, yet Hamlet (IV) now discarded the sardonic Cold War cliché. Now Radziwilowicz was himself, just another modern actor in another fawn coat stepped in from a Krakow street. 'Fortinbras' was unrecognizably thoughtful, as if re-tempered by Hamlet's experiences –

or those of the actors' generation. He crouched by the body and talked to dead Hamlet just as Hamlet confided in the skull.

And Hamlet stood up.

Budzisz-Krzyzanowska rose and walked briskly out, and suddenly on the main stage Claudius and his court were alive again, celebrating the coronation. This cyclic vision seemed truly absurdist, yet was not so. Radziwilowicz took off his coat, to reveal a black doublet. He sat at the mirror and began to speak the Prince's opening lines. *Hamlet* had begun again.

As the post-war world order changed outside the building, Wajda's shock ending argued that though all victories against the lie are provisional, each woman and man must at some point be prepared to be Hamlet – history and belief demand it – whether in 'life' or 'theatre', and how, indeed, do we divorce them?

In 1930 Meyerhold directed his wife Zinaida Raikh in Yuri Olesha's play *A List of Blessings*, which strangely parallels Wajda's production. Raikh played a Moscow actress in the Stalin era whose most famous role is Hamlet and who is riven by divided loyalties. This character was also partly based on a great dissident Soviet (male) Hamlet – Michael Chekhov – but she dies slandered, despised, and forgotten in a Paris street. A crowd of hunger marchers sweeps past her corpse, and she has no Horatio to tell her story. At the Stary Theatre in 1989 Fortinbras did learn from Hamlet's integrity; in an atomised dissolving world, a line of ethical succession carried on.

The Woman and the Wall

Though both director and the actress downplayed or even denied the feminist element in *Hamlet (IV)*, there was a tradition behind its foregrounding of a woman's consciousness. The national symbol Polonia – like Mother Russia – denotes a feminine concept of nationhood, and Wajda actually left rehearsals to rush to Warsaw during one political crisis, saying 'The Motherland's in danger.'

Hamlet became a national icon when Budzisz-Krzyzanowska assumed the pensive attitude of the Polish Christ of the Sorrows, but this also occurred in the opening image of bereavement when she sat, still and remote, under the mourning veil to mark the transition into the play, and the actress became Hamlet *via* grief. She evoked the fact that very often in Polish history the death of the father (or the exile of the son) demanded strength and leadership from the women left behind. The woman in mourning black and the hero-virgin – like Emilia Plater, 'immortalized' by Mickiewicz for fighting in the 1831 Rising – were common cultural images. Budzisz-Krzyzanowska's Hamlet evolved from one to the other, at whatever cost.

Such allusions were not irrelevant in modern Poland, especially amongst the opposition, and especially since so much of it was Catholic. The female sphere was acknowledged to be crucial: the domestic world had had to preserve national identity during invasions, partition, repression, and the modern split between state and people. Hamlet's dressing-room is the private sphere, opposed to the stark actuality outside the window and to the official fantasies of Claudius's public space.

The high level of female education in Poland is relevant too: because of the emphasis on scientific and technical training for men (to enhance the heavy-industrial base) women after 1945 had to fill the administrative class, education, and other 'caring' professions (though, like Hamlet, they rarely achieved high promotion) and were perhaps educated into dissent. The role of women in the intelligentsia (often informed by French ideas) reasserted its importance under Martial Law.

So originally Budzisz-Krzyzanowska was to be the only one to speak Baranczak's authentic and contemporary language; and so her video monitors made the audience literally share the woman's perspective as television became the inquisitorial eye instead of, as in Martial Law for instance, the tool of state ideology.

This use of the camera emphasizes the connection between the Krakow *Hamlet* and Krzystina Janda's film-maker in Wajda's *Man of Marble*, the woman who exposes official lies about post-war history. Yet the analogue imposes a different perspective on *Hamlet (IV)*. In both the play and the film a man takes over from the female lead and inherits the responsibility for changing the system – in fact the *same* man, Jerzy Radziwilowicz.

In both he is transformed by the woman's struggles and insight (he plays both the Man of Marble himself, an honest but baffled 'fifties 'shockworker' who helps create the workers' state, and his bitter activist son), but he is then equipped for action. *Hamlet (IV)*'s tiny, self-selective audience was a microcommunity united against Claudius, just as the Polish opposition was a negative alliance that could only survive through shared distrust of the system.

And as some Czech women activists in the Charter 77 movement were to say after the Velvet Revolution, 'When we were dissidents, the men needed us.' Or, to quote a Polish voice after the fall of communism, 'Polish democracy is a masculine democracy.' In the early 1980s, 23 per cent of the members of the Polish parliament, the Sejm, were women; in 1989 it was 13 per cent; after the 1991 elections, only nine per cent. And when the production opened, the future of women in post-communist Poland was already in question because of pressures from the Church for anti-abortion legislation.

Though Poland appointed its first woman Prime Minister in 1992 (Hannah Suchocka), many thought she only emerged because of her opposition to abortion – while in the previous year the (female) Under-Secretary of State for Women was forced from office on the reproductive rights issue, and the

post was abolished. And there was another irony: *Hamlet (IV)* could not survive in the theatrical market economy whose birth it helped to herald. 'It was a deficit production', as the actress put it later, only possible in a system of total subsidy.

But in the process of playing it, she felt she had made discoveries about the play and herself, and we must end on that upnote. For Wajda had firm ideas about the shape of the production beforehand, of course, and – startlingly for Polish theatre – the rehearsal period could only be five weeks because, as she said wryly, it was 'presold' to America:

> He's a conman of genius. I was convinced that we'd take ages to work on it, and in fact it was sad that it happened so quickly. To tell the truth, the first performances in New York weren't good, because we were terribly underconfident, I felt too shy to act. I hadn't yet found myself in there. I was a little afraid it would be shallow, absurd, that no-one would understand my intentions, that I'd be accused of exhibitionism. I can't specify the moment when I felt it made sense. The meanings are so rich that every night you can discover new things. And that's how it grew with me. Until I decided I could try it forever.

Notes

Quotations from Teresa Budzisz-Krzyzanowska are from an interview with her in Warsaw, translated by Barbara Plebanek, who made this essay possible. Quotations from Wajda are taken from his book, *A Double Vision* (London, 1990), and from the Stary programme for *Hamlet (IV)*, which printed extracts from his correspondence with Baranczak. The production was received at first with little enthusiasm in Poland, perhaps because the political events were so attention-seizing – though *Dialog* magazine published an extensive analysis (No. 6, 1990) – but it has slowly, and rightfully, assumed the status of a classic.

David Bradby

Bernard-Marie Koltès:
Chronology, Contexts, Connections

The plays of Bernard-Marie Koltès have been phenomenally successful, not just in Europe, but worldwide – his last work before his death in 1989, *Roberto Zucco*, having been performed in seventeen countries. Despite an early production of *Twilight Zone* by Pierre Audi at the Almeida Theatre in 1981, English appreciation has been tardy, but now this situation is set to change, with the Royal Court Theatre commissioning Martin Crimp to make a translation of *Roberto Zucco*, to be directed by James Macdonald, and Methuen bringing out a volume of Koltès's plays. These present a unique fusion of the French classical tradition combined with Shakespeare (he translated *The Winter's Tale* into French) and modern influences such as Genet and Fugard (he also translated *The Blood Knot*). After his death, Giles Croft wrote of Koltès: 'He considered himself an outsider, rootless, and this perception of himself is reflected in his characters, whose tragedy is their inability to connect with one another, often despite their ability to articulate their despair. He created dark, mythic, polyglot worlds where people are dwarfed by or divorced from their surroundings: hotel rooms, construction sites, quaysides.' Koltès's career was closely linked with that of Patrice Chéreau, who produced all his major plays, and who performed in his own production of *In The Solitude of the Cotton Fields* at last year's Edinburgh Festival. Here, David Bradby, Professor of Drama at Royal Holloway, University of London, contributes his own assessments of both men's life and work, to complement full chronological and bibliographical details of Koltès's career.

Bernard-Marie Koltès, 1948–1989

KOLTÈS'S life, on the surface at least, contained none of the deadly struggles that characterize his plays. He was not one to man the barricades or put out slogans, even during his student days in the late 1960s. In fact he tended to avoid conflict whenever possible; though homosexual, he never 'came out', or aligned himself with gay liberation movements, and the fact that he was suffering from AIDS was a closely guarded secret for most of the 1980s.

This was not from lack of courage on his part, but rather from a kind of natural reserve: he had no desire to serve as a rallying cry or to get caught up in fashionable causes. In this, as in many other ways, he resembled Genet, who campaigned in favour of the Black Panthers and the Palestine Liberation Organization but kept his distance from political or social struggles in France. He was born and brought up in Metz, a

barrack town in the Eastern part of France, where his father was a professional soldier. He had two older brothers, Jean-Marie and François. His grandparents on both sides of the family were local people, miners and foresters, whose family memories stretched back to the time when Alsace-Lorraine had been annexed by the Germans. His mother was a fervent Catholic: her sons were given Catholic names and were sent, not to the state school, but to the catholic college in the centre of Metz.

For most of the 1950s, the father was absent in Algeria, so his children saw little of him, but their teachers would have left them in no doubt that the conflict in Algeria had a crusading side to it, representing the struggle of Christian France against the forces of Islam. This was the last and bitterest of France's colonial wars. In the eyes of the vast majority of the population,

Algeria was not a separate country at all, but part of France that happened to be situated on the other side of the Mediterranean. The struggle against the FLN (Algerian National Liberation Front) was seen as a fight to preserve the integrity of the nation in much the same way as opposing the IRA in Northern Ireland has seemed, to many British people, to be about preserving the United Kingdom. It was a conflict which would later have a central place in Koltès's plays.

At the end of the 1950s a group of army generals staged an attempted coup against the French government in their last-ditch attempt to prevent Algeria being granted independence. They were out-manoeuvred by the superior political skill of de Gaulle, who had recently become president and had inaugurated the Fifth Republic. In 1960 General Massu, one of the ringleaders, was recalled to Metz, where he was given the post of military governor to keep him occupied. Koltès recalled the mixture of fear and fascination he felt as Massu's paratroopers marched through the streets.

In the two years that remained until the peace agreements of Evian brought the conflict to an end, there was constant tension in Metz, which sometimes erupted into pitched street-battles between 'paras' and Arabs. One night there was a major disorder that left seventeen Arabs dead. In order to try to contain the situation, the Prefect decreed a no-go area for French people in the part of town where most of the Arabs lived, thus effectively creating a ghetto. This had a considerable effect on the lives of the young Koltès brothers, since the school they attended was situated in the no-go area. The territoriality that was to be so important a part of Koltès's plays can be traced back to these early experiences.

After secondary school, Bernard-Marie went on to study at the School of Journalism in Strasbourg. He was an accomplished pianist, and continued to take lessons after the move to Strasbourg. One teacher who particularly influenced him was an expert in the music of Messian, and for a while he planned a career as a professional organist. But everything changed for him in 1968.

This was the year in which a near-revolution swept through France and universities up and down the country were occupied by students. The Strasbourg faculty hall had a particularly fine grand piano and throughout the May of 1968 François remembers his brother seated at this piano filling the hall with the music of Bach, Liszt, and Messian.

But the real change in the future playwright's life came when he discovered for the first time the pleasures of travel, going first to Paris and then, in the same year, to New York City. For the twenty-year-old boy, brought up in a protective Catholic family and used to life in the French provinces, the discovery of New York, especially of its black population, affected him deeply. He developed a passion for black music, idolizing Billie Holiday and Otis Redding, and returned frequently to New York, which became the setting for *Quai Ouest*, one of his major plays.

On his return to France, he began to write plays, and abandoned the study of classical music. Throughout the 1970s he lived from hand to mouth, taking all kinds of temporary jobs to pay the rent. His favourite was taking tickets at the cinema, because this allowed him to indulge his passion for films. He said later that, no matter how bad the film, he always found something interesting in cinema, whereas most of the time he found theatre unbearable.

Inspired by his first visit to the theatre, when he had seen Maria Casarès playing the title role in Seneca's *Medea*, his early plays were intensely theatrical. All were adaptations, because he saw them as apprentice pieces through which he was learning his craft. His appetite for reading, especially the Russian classics, emerges in the models he chose to adapt for his early plays – Gorky's *My Childhood* and Dostoevsky's *Crime and Punishment* among them.

Within four years Koltès had written six plays, four of which he staged with a group of friends in a student theatre in Strasbourg, and two of which were broadcast on both local and national radio (the first with Maria Casarès in the title role). He also attracted the attention of Hubert Gignoux, a veteran

Bernard-Marie Koltès: a Chronology

1948   9 April, birth of Bernard-Marie Koltès at Metz, a town in the Eastern part of France. His father, a professional soldier, was away in Algeria for much of the 1950s.

1958-62   Koltès's secondary schooling began against a background of bombings and disturbances as the crisis of the Algerian conflict pushed France to the brink of civil war.

1967   After completing school in Metz, Koltès went to Strasbourg, where he attended courses at the School of Journalism. He also studied music, and even considered becoming a professional organist.

1968   In January he saw Maria Casarès at Strasbourg, playing the central role in Seneca's *Medea*; this was his first visit to a theatre and had a profound effect on him. During the May 1968 occupations of colleges and factories Koltès avoided political involvement. In the Summer he travelled to Paris, and then to New York.

1969   First attempt at writing for the theatre: a stage adaptation of Gorky's *My Childhood*, entitled *Les Amertumes* (*Bitternesses*). He sent the play to Hubert Gignoux, director of the Strasbourg National Drama School, asking for advice.

1970   Koltès directed a few friends in a production of his play at the Théâtre du Quai, Strasbourg (performances in May and June). Hubert Gignoux saw the production and invited Koltès to join his course in the *régie* (technical) section of the School. He joined, but dropped out during his second year.

1971   He wrote and directed his second and third plays in the same little student Théâtre du Quai: *La Marche* (*The March*), based on the Song of Songs, and *Procès Ivre* (*Drunken Trial*), based on Dostoevsky's *Crime and Punishment*.

1972   *L'Héritage* (*The Inheritance*) broadcast on local Radio-Alsace and then on France Culture (produced by Lucien Attoun) with Maria Casarès.

1973   *Récits morts* (*Dead Stories*) directed by Koltès at the Théâtre du Quai. During the 1970s Koltès earned little or nothing from his writing and took casual jobs (e.g., selling tickets in Strasbourg cinemas).

1974   A second play, *Des Voix sourdes* (*Deaf/Muffled Voices*), broadcast, first on Radio Alsace and afterwards on France Culture:

1975-76   Koltès moved to Paris and wrote his first novel, *La Fuite à cheval très loin dans la ville* (*The Flight on Horseback far into the Town*), dated September 1976. The typescript circulated among friends for some years before being published by Les Editions de Minuit in 1984.

1977   Wrote a dramatic monologue, *La Nuit juste avant les forêts* (*The Night just before the Forests*) for actor Yves Ferry (whom he had known at the Strasbourg Drama School) and directed him in a performance given on the fringe of the Avignon Theatre Festival. Invited by Bruno Boeglin to observe a series of actors' workshops based on the stories of J. D. Salinger and to write a play inspired by them, he wrote *Sallinger* (sic), directed by Boeglin and performed during the 1977-78 season at his El Dorado theatre in Lyon.

1978   Journey to West Africa, where he visited friends working on a construction site in Nigeria.

1979   Returned to West Africa, visiting Mali and Ivory Coast; six-month trip to Nicaragua (just before the Sandanista revolution) and to Guatemala, during which he wrote *Combat de nègre et de chiens* (*Struggle of the Dogs and the Black*). The play was published as a 'tapuscrit' by Théâtre Ouvert – i.e., one of a limited number of typescripts made for circulation among theatre professionals so as to encourage the dissemination of new theatre writing.

1980   Radio broadcast on France Culture of *Combat de nègre et de chiens*. The text received its first commercial publication in the 'Théâtre Ouvert' series of Stock (Paris) together with *La Nuit juste avant les forêts*.

of the decentralization movement, who was at this time head of the National Drama School situated in Strasbourg. Gignoux attended Koltès's first play and, on the strength of this, invited him to join the School, in the technical department.

Koltès did so, and maintained a friendly relationship with Gignoux for the rest of his life, although he dropped out of the course, preferring to devote his mental energies to writing and staging his plays. He would always show drafts of his plays to Gignoux, and Gignoux was responsible for bringing him to the attention of others working in the theatre, notably Lucien Attoun, director of 'Théâtre Ouvert', and Patrice Chéreau, who directed all but one of Koltès's major plays in the 1980s.

Lucien Attoun, who runs 'Théâtre Ouvert' with his wife Micheline, is a broadcaster, publisher, and entrepreneur of experimental theatre. He produced the first two national radio broadcasts of plays by Koltès and published his first dramatic monologue, *The Night just before the Forests*, together with *Struggle of the Dogs and the Black*, in 1980. For most of the 1970s, however, Koltès found it hard to establish himself as a professional playwright. His response was a characteristic one: he decided to move away from Strasbourg, leaving behind his network of theatre contacts there and attempting a different kind of writing. He moved into a flat in Paris and wrote a novel (untranslated as yet) *La Fuite à cheval très loin dans la ville*.

But in 1977 he was tempted back to theatre work. In this year he met Bruno Boeglin, a theatre director who had a group of actors developing improvisations on themes taken from the writings of J. D. Salinger. Boeglin shared his passion for travel and, especially, his growing interest in South America, which both men were to visit in the following years. Koltès spent some time watching Boeglin's company at work, and then, drawing on their improvisations, wrote *Sallinger* (sic), which was performed by Boeglin's company in Lyon during the following season.

At the request of Yves Ferry, an actor whom he had known since they were both at the Strasbourg drama school, he also wrote a dramatic monologue, which he regarded as his first truly original play. This was *The Night just before the Forests* (originally *The Night just before the Forests of Nicaragua*). Koltès directed Ferry in its first performance at the Avignon Festival of 1977. The play was well received by the critics, and this experience, as also his participation in the work of Bruno Boeglin's company, gave Koltès renewed belief in his powers as a playwright.

During the next two years he travelled extensively in Africa and South America, becoming especially interested in the civil war in Nicaragua. Two stories that he wrote in Nicaragua in 1978 have recently been published, and reveal his ability to create a compelling stream-of-consciousness prose style, evoking the mentalities of people caught up in a struggle for survival in places where armed squads roam the night, but where even the most destitute people have their heads filled with dreams of fabulous American wealth. These stories are reminiscent of Bruce Chatwin and his ability to bring places alive though the eyes of a traveller. Koltès had the idea for *Struggle of the Dogs and the Black* when staying in a camp in Nigeria: the cries of the guards in the night provided his first inspiration. The play was later written in the course of a six-month stay in Guatemala.

About this time he also saw productions by Patrice Chéreau, and decided that he wanted Chéreau to be the one to produce his plays. This meant that *Struggle* had to wait three years for its first French production, since Chéreau was at this time negotiating his move from the Théâtre National Populaire in Villeurbanne (where he had been co-artistic director with Roger Planchon in the 1970s) to his own theatre, the Théâtre des Amandiers, at Nanterre in the northern industrial suburbs of Paris. In the meantime, Koltès travelled back and forth between Paris and New York, and it was here that Françoise Kourilsky produced the world premiere of the play (in English translation) at the experimental La Mama in 1979.

The 1980s were for Bernard-Marie Koltès a time of both fulfilment and frustration. On

1981 Four-month visit to New York. Koltès beginning to be known in theatre circles: *La Nuit juste avant les forêts* revived at the Petit Odéon with the actor Richard Fontana. Received a commission for a play by the Comédie Française. Plans made with Françoise Kourilsky for a production of *Combat de nègre et de chiens* in New York.

1982 Returned to New York for world premiere of *Combat de nègre et de chiens* at Theatre La Mama: the English translation, by Matthew Ward, was originally entitled *Come Dog, Come Night*: at Koltès's insistence, it was later changed to *Struggle of the Dogs and the Black* and published under this title, first in the collection of the New York Ubu Repertory Theatre (1982), later by Methuen in *New French Plays* (1989). Koltès translated Athol Fugard's *The Blood Knot* for production at the Avignon Festival.

1983 Patrice Chéreau opened his new Théâtre des Amandiers at Nanterre (on the outskirts of Paris) with the French premiere of *Combat de nègre et de chiens*. The set (by Richard Peduzzi) was monumental and the cast star-studded: Michel Piccoli, Philippe Léotard, Myriam Boyer, Sidiki Bakaba: the critics were mostly enthusiastic. Until his death at the end of the decade, Koltès was widely accepted as the most important new voice in French theatre. From this point on he was able to live from his writing, though he earned more from foreign (especially German) productions than from the exploitation of his work in France. Worked briefly as dramaturge with François Regnault on Chéreau's production of *Les Paravents* (*The Screens*) by Jean Genet; together they published *La Famille des Orties* (*The Nettle Family*).

1984 Journey to Senegal. Publication of *La Nuit juste avant les forêts* (see 1977). Four different productions of *Combat de nègre et de chiens* in German theatres (Frankfurt, Tübingen, Wuppertal, and Munich).

1985 Publication of *Quai ouest* by Editions de Minuit; world premiere of the play given in Dutch at the Publiekstheater, Amsterdam.

1986 French premiere of *Quai ouest*, directed by Patrice Chéreau, with Maria Casarès in the cast, at the Théâtre des Amandiers. The critics were again impressed by the writing, but blamed Chéreau and Peduzzi for crushing the play beneath a monumental production. Koltès responded to a commission by the Avignon Festival for a play in a series with the title 'Oser aimer' ('To Dare to Love'), with the short play *Tabataba*, about someone who 'dares to love' his motorcycle. Publication of *Dans la solitude des champs de coton* (*In the Solitude of the Cotton Fields*) by Minuit.

1987 First production of *Dans la solitude des champs de coton* by Patrice Chéreau at Nanterre. The role of the Client was taken by Laurent Malet and that of the Dealer by Isaach de Bankolé. In subsequent seasons Chéreau revived this production, taking the role of the Dealer himself; this provoked a temporary break with Koltès, who insisted that he had written the role of the Dealer for a black actor.

1988 Two major firsts for Koltès: *Le Retour au désert* (*Return to the Desert*) received its premiere in a production by Patrice Chéreau at the Théâtre du Rond-Point in the centre of Paris. Jacqueline Maillan, a popular comic actress for whom he had written it, was in the central role and Michel Piccoli played her brother. At the Théâtre des Amandiers his translation of *The Winter's Tale* was directed by Luc Bondy. In the metro, Koltès was struck by police 'wanted' posters with photos of the murderer Roberto Succo, and became interested in his case, especially after he had seen television pictures of Succo's last hours on the roof-top of an Italian prison.

1989 15 April, death of Koltès in Paris a week after his forty-first birthday. Shortly before his death, he had completed his final play, *Roberto Zucco*.

1990 World premiere of *Roberto Zucco*, directed by Peter Stein at the Berlin Schaubühne.

the one hand he developed a close working relationship with Patrice Chéreau, who committed himself to producing every new work that Koltès wrote. On the other hand, Koltès was upset to find that his plays were produced more abroad than in France (his financial independence during the last years of his life was largely due to royalties from

German theatres), and that the productions often seemed wilfully to flout his intentions. Chéreau's production of *Struggle of the Dogs and the Black* was a huge critical success in France, but did not give rise to other productions, and this neglect was set to continue until after his death. It seemed that other directors were too much in awe of Chéreau and did not wish to risk unflattering comparisons with stagings of their own.

Nevertheless, the unequivocal support of a major director such as Chéreau was certainly a factor in his greater confidence and increased output during this period. Equally important to him was being part of a professional producing company, for which he did other, occasional work. For example, in 1983 he had a brief spell working on Chéreau's production of Genet's play *The Screens,* and in 1987 he made a translation of Shakespeare's *The Winter's Tale,* which was directed at the Théâtre des Amandiers by Luc Bondy. Koltès said in an interview that he had enjoyed this greatly, and would like to translate another, perhaps *Richard III* or *Lear.*

Towards the end of his life, he appeared to be moving away from the neoclassical respect for the three unities that had characterized his early plays, and towards a much greater freedom in the use of dramatic form, a freedom he said he had learned from Shakespeare. This new-found freedom is visible for the first time in *Return to the Desert,* written in 1988.

From 1975 until his death, Koltès had a flat in Paris. He never felt the need to identify with a particular community, valuing the freedom to travel above everything. He wrote that he lacked all feeling for 'home', but experienced something of the comfort and security normally associated with home when he listened to Bob Marley. One of his favourite Marley songs, 'Running Away', sums up the restlessness and desire for escape that were a central part of Koltès's spiritual make-up.

In the last year of his life his freedom of movement was severely curtailed by his physical condition. He compensated for this by writing his last play, *Roberto Zucco,* about a man who escaped from both high security jails and the normal restrictions imposed by life in society. Although Zucco is presented as a monster, he is also depicted as compellingly attractive and very articulate when he chooses – not unlike Brecht's Baal. His combination of detachment and escapism, articulacy and self-denigration, anguished isolation together with a horror of society, make it tempting to see in him the spiritual self-portrait of the author and a summation of his view of himself *vis-à-vis* society.

Patrice Chéreau

PATRICE CHÉREAU, born in 1944, is one of a young generation of directors who came to prominence in France after the upheavals of 1968. He is known for his bold reinterpretations of outsize works, such as Wagner's *Ring* cycle and Ibsen's *Peer Gynt,* and for the extraordinary visual quality of his productions, due in part to his long collaboration with the Italian designer Richard Peduzzi.

From the start of his career, when he formed a student company, Chéreau's work has always been characterized by its visual brilliance. Not only are his designs striking in themselves, but they also cast a harsh, new light on the authors he chooses to direct. Thus Labiche (*L'Affaire de la rue Lourcine,* 1966); Shakespeare (*Richard II,* 1970); Marivaux (*The Dispute,* 1973); Wagner (*The Ring,* 1976-80); Ibsen (*Peer Gynt,* 1981): all were presented in visual terms that surprised and shocked their audiences. Without sacrificing the elements of playfulness in these works, Chéreau succeeded in providing them with new, stark outlines, suitable for a post-Artaudian age. His designs were at first all done by himself, but from 1970 onwards he began to collaborate with Richard Peduzzi, who designed all his subsequent productions. The stability of this working collaboration, together with the

Productions by Patrice Chéreau

In collaboration with Jean-Pierre Vincent, Groupe Théâtral Louis-le-Grand

Henry Monnier, *Scènes Populaires*, 1964
Victor Hugo, *L'Intervention*, 1964
Lope de Vega, *Fuente Ovejuna*, 1965
Marivaux, *L'Héritier de Village*, 1965
Labiche, *L'Affaire de la rue Lourcine*, 1966

Compagnie Patrice Chéreau, Théâtre de Sartrouville

Lenz, *Les Soldats*, 1967
Kuan Han Ching, *La Neige au milieu de l'été; Le Voleur de femmes*, 1967
Dimitriadis, *Le Prix de la révolte au marché noir*, 1968
Molière, *Dom Juan*, 1969

Freelance

Shakespeare, *Richard II*, Marseille, then Paris, 1970
Pablo Neruda, adapt. Chéreau, *Splendore et morte di Joaquin Murieta*, Milan, 1970
Tankred Dorst, *Toller*, Milan, 1970
Marivaux, *La Finta Serva*, Spoleto, 1971
Wedekind, *Lulu*, Milan, 1972

Théâtre National Populaire, Villeurbanne

Marlowe, *Le Massacre à Paris*, 1972
Tankred Dorst, *Toller*, 1973
Marivaux, *La Dispute*, 1973

Edward Bond, *Lear*, 1975
Jean-Paul Wenzel, *Loin d'Hagondange*, 1977
Ibsen, *Peer Gynt*, 1981

Théâtre des Amandiers, Nanterre

Bernard-Marie Koltès, *Combat de Nègre et de chiens*, 1983
Jean Genet, *Les Paravents*, 1983
Heiner Müller, *Quartett*, 1985
Bernard-Marie Koltès, *Quai Ouest*, 1986
Bernard-Marie Koltès, *Dans la solitude des champs de coton*, 1987. Revived 1995
Chekhov, *Platonov*, 1987
Bernard-Marie Koltès, *Le Retour au désert*, Paris (Rond-Point), 1988
Shakespeare, *Hamlet*, 1988

Opera

Rossini, *L'Italiana in Algeri*, Spoleto, 1969
Offenbach, *Les Contes d'Hoffmann*, Paris, 1974
Wagner, *Ring Cycle*, Bayreuth, 1976-80
Berg, *Lulu*, Paris, 1979
Mozart, *Lucio Silla*, Paris 1984

Bibliography

Les Voies de la Création Théâtrale, XIV: Patrice Chéreau, Paris: C.N.R.S., 1986.
Théâtre en Europe, No. 17, July 1988 (Paris: Editions Beba).

considerable talents of Jacques Schmidt's costumes and André Diot's lighting designs, have ensured stylistic consistency and boldness in all Chéreau's work.

His career has been an uneven one: after student productions, he ran the Théâtre de Sartrouville from 1966 until 1969, when it went bankrupt. He then worked for a short period under Strehler at the Piccolo Teatro of Milan, before being taken on by Roger Planchon as a co-director of the newly designated Théâtre National Populaire in Villeurbanne. Chéreau's production of Marlowe's *Massacre at Paris* was chosen to open the new theatre in 1972.

Set on a stage which gradually filled with water in the course of the evening, the performance was memorable for the images of warring factions wading through the blood of their victims. His second production at Villeurbanne was an equally memorable staging of Marivaux's *The Dispute* (1973), in which the erotic games of four teenagers were viewed as if through the eyes of de Sade. *Peer Gynt* in 1981 was his last production for the Théâtre National Populaire: played uncut over two evenings, it was the theatrical equivalent of the work he had embarked on at Bayreuth five years earlier with his *Ring* cycle (musical director: Pierre Boulez). In these two mammoth productions, with the help of his design team, he set the nineteenth century's concern with the myth of individual freedom against the background of the industrial and mercantile revolutions of that century.

At the same time as directing such major works, Chéreau always concerned himself with modern writers. He was responsible for two striking productions of Tankred Dorst's play *Toller* at the Piccolo Teatro (1970) and at the Théâtre National Populaire (1973). While at Villeurbanne, he directed *Far from Hagondange* (1977) by the young French playwright Jean-Paul Wenzel, and after 1982, when he became artistic director of the Théâtre des Amandiers at Nanterre, championed Koltès's cause, producing four of his major texts: *Struggle of the Dogs and the Black* (1983); *Western Dock* (1986); *In the Solitude of the Cotton Fields* (1987); *Return to the Desert* (1988). His period at Nanterre was also notable for a revival of Genet's *The Screens* (1983) and a production of Heiner Müller's *Quartet* (1985). While director at Nanterre, he also set up an acting school, and it was with the students of this school that he directed his first play by Chekhov, *Platonov* (1987).

In the course of the 1980s he also began directing films, and one of these (*L'Homme blessé*, 1983) met with considerable critical acclaim. But some critics accused him of crushing the theatre texts he directed under the weight of over-ambitious décors that would have been more suitable for film, and in *Struggle of the Dogs and the Black*, for example, set on a West African building site, he had a realistic concrete road bridge and real cars driving on stage.

Chéreau became a target (along with Planchon and several others) for critics who claimed that theatres were too highly subsidized and wasted their money on unnecessarily expensive sets. Since the end of the decade, when he resigned from the Théâtre des Amandiers, he has worked free-lance, spending the greater part of his time directing films. In 1995 his film *La Reine Margot* enjoyed wide critical acclaim. In it, he returns to the subject of Marlowe's *Massacre at Paris*, now using a Dumas novel as his source. The film included well-known star actors such as Isabelle Adjani and Daniel Auteuil, and was characterized by a restless and constantly mobile camera, whose patterns of movement matched the complexity of the courtly intrigues of the plot.

Koltès: the Major Plays

The Night just before the Forests

This is the play that Koltès described as his first original work for theatre (after the seven apprentice pieces, all adapted from other texts, which he had written in the early 1970s). It is a sixty-page dramatic monologue spoken by a young Arab man living in a French city and addressed to the person who has picked him up or has offered him a room for the night – it is never entirely clear which. He talks of life in the poor district of town, living among the prostitutes and down-and-outs, coping with all the misery of existence on the bread-line in a French city slum.

He also talks of the racial abuse he encounters and the permanent state of fear in which he lives. The details of his circumstances have a deadly accuracy, describing what life is like for the immigrant under-class in France, but his precise circumstances are left vague, so that we are never sure exactly where the encounter takes place. Although his experience is that of a victim, the more he talks, the more a kind of innocence and strength emerges from the way he approaches the world, and the overall effect on an audience is of a painfully truthful but somehow invigorating experience, having to face a world view that is familiar yet strange at the same time.

The play was first performed by Yves Ferry at the Avignon Festival in 1977, directed by the author. It received a good press, and was revived several times, including a highly praised production by Jean-Luc Boutté at the Odéon's studio theatre in 1981, with Richard Fontana performing. It was also the first of Koltès's plays to be seen in Britain, in a translation by Peter Cox entitled *Twilight Zone*, produced by Pierre Audi for the Edinburgh Festival in 1981 and revived at the Almeida Theatre, London, shortly afterwards.

Struggle of the Dogs and the Black

What is the value of a man's life? Is a European more valuable than an African, or an engineer more useful than a labourer? These are the questions at the centre of this play. It starts with Alboury's simple statement: 'I have come for the body.' The body he wants is that of a dead worker, Alboury's brother, who has been killed on the West African construction site where a road bridge is being built, financed by European capital. Horn, the site manager, tries to make a deal with him: he offers him first whisky, then financial compensation, then tries to put Alboury off with promises that the body will be returned to his village the next morning. But Alboury refuses to be put off and settles down to wait.

In the confrontation between Horn and Alboury, Koltès presents the conflict of two opposed world views: Horn is logical, managerial, sure of himself and of his ability to get things done; Alboury is patient yet tenacious, with an attitude towards the world that puts a high priority on respect for the dead. For Horn, a man is worth what he can achieve when alive; for Alboury he takes his place in the natural cycle of the unborn, the living, and the dead.

Horn, meanwhile, is trying to cope with pressures from the other characters in the play. There are only two: the first is Léone, a young woman whom Horn has met on a recent trip to Paris, and who has been persuaded to come out and visit him. She is suffering from a combination of travel sickness and culture shock, and refuses to come out of the bungalow, but perhaps her main reason for shutting herself in is uncertainty about what is expected of her. The other is Cal; he is half Horn's age, a French engineer employed on the project. In the course of the play he reveals himself to be racist, self-pitying, and violent (the only affection he

feels is for his dog). It slowly emerges that he is responsible for the death of the African worker and that he has dumped the body in a panic. In the end he is shot, presumably by one of the African guards whose presence is audible just offstage throughout the play.

The play's twenty short scenes are made up almost exclusively of encounters between just two out of the four characters. By varying the permutations, Koltès builds up a pattern of attraction and repulsion, desire and disgust, and reveals the ideological, political, and economic foundations of the assumptions on which the characters base their behaviour. The form in which they express themselves is a mixture of dialogue and extended monologue. The style is strongly reminiscent of Faulkner (a writer to whom Koltès acknowledged his debt). Like the monologues of Faulkner's characters, they focus on concrete, closely observed details, and they employ a language that is not remote from that of ordinary speech, yet posseses the complex, condensed quality of language in dreams, and lacks the realistic patina of banal everyday talk.

The setting has a crucial role to play: the stage direction describes it as a construction site, somewhere in West Africa, surrounded by fences and observation towers, with housing for the site supervisors, clumps of bougainvillaea, a van pulled up under a tree, and a half-finished bridge consisting of two concrete columns rising up from a sea of mud. The darkness, and the fact that the camp is surrounded by armed guards, lends tension and suspense to a plot that has been set in motion by the death of one man and will end with the death of another. The violent atmosphere, the strained relationships between Africans and Europeans, the fact that work on the project has come to a standstill and that there are hints of financial corruption – all combine to undermine the value of such engineering projects funded by western capital.

Koltès claimed, however, that the play was not primarily about the effect of neo-colonialist economic policies within Black Africa, but rather about 'France and the Whites: something seen from a distance may become easier to decipher.' (See under 'Africa', page 88.) By this he meant that the play focuses on the construction of European cultural identities. This emerged powerfully in the production by Chéreau, thanks to compelling performances by Michel Piccoli in the role of Horn and Philippe Léotard as Cal.

The play's world premiere, at the La Mama theatre of New York, was produced by Françoise Kourilsky. Shortly before this, Kourilsky had set up the Ubu Repertory Theatre in New York, funded by French government subsidy, with the purpose of providing a shop window in America for new French playwrights. Koltès's fascination with New York made it inevitable that he would meet Kourilsky, and she was keen to make his work known in the USA. The translation, by Matthew Ward, succeeded in capturing some of the quality of Koltès's original style, but contained inaccuracies. This first production was a relatively small-scale affair, and there is no record of what Koltès felt about it.

The first production in France, however, was a different matter. For the opening production of his directorship at the Théâtre des Amandiers in 1983, Patrice Chéreau wanted to make a splash, and he succeeded. He brought with him to Nanterre the Italian designer Richard Peduzzi, whith whom he had already worked for more than a decade, both in Lyon at the Théâtre National Populaire, and at the Bayreuth theatre for the famous staging of Wagner's *Ring* cycle, conducted by Pierre Boulez. His design followed the stage directions closely, with two unfinished concrete bridge supports rising out of sight and clumps of bushes planted in the heaps of sand and rubble strewn across the stage. But instead of the bungalow, there was a caravan, towed on and off stage by a car at various stages of the action.

The parts of Horn and Cal were taken by Michel Piccoli and Philippe Léotard, two actors well-known to French audiences, especially from their work for the cinema. Léona was performed by Myriam Boyer and Alboury by Sidiki Bakaba. The play was favourably received by the critics, who were unanimous in their praise for all aspects of the production – acting, design, and direction – as well as for the text.

The play was quickly taken up by theatres in Germany, with four productions (at Frankfurt, Tübingen, Wuppertal, and Munich) before the end of 1984, and a further eighteen in the ensuing ten years. The first production in England was by Michael Batz at the Gate Theatre, Notting Hill, in 1986. The Scottish premiere was at the Traverse, Edinburgh, for the Edinburgh International Festival in 1991, directed by Andrew Farrell. Both productions used the translation by Matthew Ward, which was published by Methuen in *New French Plays* (1989). A new translation by David Bradby and Maria M. Delgado, entitled *Black Battles with Dogs*, is to be published by Methuen in 1997.

Western Dock

In a disused riverside warehouse in New York, Maurice Koch, a rich elderly man, tries to bargain with some down-and-outs to ensure the success of his suicide attempt. The setting is emblematic of Koch and the civilization he represents: it is a place that has been built by the economic forces that made him rich and, in its heyday, had a certain vitality. Now it is a wasteland, devoid of life and inhabited only by people whose status is on the margins of legality.

The play charts events through two nights and the intervening day as the inhabitants of this marginal territory try to make something out of the arrival of Koch and his luxury car, while also settling old scores amongst themselves. They include a family of illegal immigrants from South America, and two unattached young men: Fak, who is Asiatic, about 22, and Abad (not his real name), black, about 30. The family consists of Rodolphe, the father, 58; Cécile, the mother, 60; Charles or Carlos, their son, 28; and Claire, their daughter, 14.

Rodolophe has been involved in a war (presumably a civil war) and has had to board a boat in a hurry; he has a Kalashnikov with him. Cécile is the character who seems most out of place; she speaks some of

Plays by Koltès: a Chronology and Bibliography

Premieres and publications, from a list by Serge Saada published in Alternatives Théâtrales, *special issue devoted to Koltès, June 1990, p. 35-6.*

Les Amertumes, adapted from Gorky's novel *Childhood*, produced by the author, Strasbourg, 1970.

La Marche, inspired by the Song of Solomon, produced by the author, Strasbourg, 1971.

Procès Ivre, inspired by Dostoevsky's novel *Crime and Punishment*, produced by the author, Strasbourg, 1971.

L'Héritage, produced on Radio-France Alsace, and then again on France-Culture (also Radio), 1972.

Récits Morts, produced by the author, Strasbourg, 1973.

Des Voix sourdes, produced on Radio-France, Alsace, and on France-Culture, 1974.

Le Jour des meurtres dans l'histoire d'Hamlet, 1974.

Sallinger, inspired by the stories of J. D. Salinger, produced by Bruno Boeglin, Lyon, 1977. Published by Minuit, 1995.

La Nuit juste avant les forêts, monologue, produced by the author, Avignon Festival, 1977. Published by Stock/Théâtre Ouvert, 1980; Minuit, 1988. First English production as *Twilight Zone*, directed by Pierre Audi, Edinburgh Festival and Almeida Theatre, 1981.

Combat de nègre et de chiens, published by Stock/Théâtre Ouvert, 1980; Minuit, 1989. First produced by Françoise Kourilsky, La Mama ETC, New York, 1982, in a translation by Matthew Ward; first French production by Patrice Chéreau, Théâtre des Amandiers, Nanterre, 1983. First English production, as *Struggle of the Black Man and the Dogs*, directed by Michael Batz, Gate Theatre, 1988. English publication: *Struggle of the Dogs and the Black*, trans. Matthew Ward, in *New French Plays* (Methuen, 1989).

Le Lien du sang, translation of *The Blood Knot* by Athol Fugard, first produced by Yutaka Wada, Avignon Festival, 1982.

Quai ouest, published by Minuit, 1985. First produced by Stephane Stroux in a Dutch translation, Amsterdam, 1985; first French production by Patrice Chéreau, Théâtre des Amandiers, 1986.

Tabataba, produced by Hammou Graia, Avignon Festival, 1986. Published by Minuit with *Roberto Zucco* (see below).

Dans la solitude des champs de coton, published by Minuit, 1986. First produced by Patrice Chéreau, Théâtre des Amandiers, 1987. Revived, Venice Biennale, 1995.

Le Conte d'hiver, translation of *The Winter's Tale* by Shakespeare, first produced by Luc Bondy, Théâtre des Amandiers, 1988. Published by Minuit, 1988.

Le Retour au désert, first produced by Patrice Chéreau, Théâtre du Rond-Point, Paris, 1988. Published by Minuit, 1988.

Roberto Zucco, first produced by Peter Stein in a German translation by Simon Werle, Schaubühne, Berlin, 1990; first French production by Bruno Boeglin, Théâtre National Populaire, Villeurbanne, 1991. Published by Minuit, with *Tabataba*, 1990.

the time in Spanish, some of the time in Quechua. She is involved in a continual and unsuccessful struggle to control her son and her daughter.

Charles resents the attempts by both his parents to keep him in their power. He spends the play attempting to do a number of deals with Fak or Abad; there is a suggestion that he and Abad have been involved in drug dealing, but the main object of attraction for Charles is the Jaguar – a 5.3 litre, 12 cylinder, Vanden Plas XJS – which fascinates him. The daughter, Claire, is being pursued by Fak, who succeeds towards the end of the play in seducing her. All the characters are linked by a variety of deals or bargains,

from the very beginning when Koch simply wants someone to help him commit suicide. There are hints that he and Monique have together been involved in embezzling funds from Koch's business.

Rodolphe's Kalashnikov passes from hand to hand and is eventually used to kill both Koch and Charles. The latter is killed by Abad, who has remained silent throughout the action. Koltès was anxious that Abad should not be seen as a passive character. He wrote, in his afterword, that 'Abad is not a negative character in the centre of the play; it is the play that is the negative of Abad.'

There is no central story as such, but a series of plots within plots, as the characters circle one another, each looking for ways to extract some advantage from the others, trying to team up, or distancing themselves from the characters they distrust. The atmosphere of simmering violence and marginality, combined with passages of reflection on the state of the world or of the characters' personal situation in it, result in much of the dialogue resembling a Tarantino screenplay. Koltès's stage directions emphasize the use of light and dark and the contrasts between scenes that take place in brilliant sunshine, while others are half hidden in the shadows.

Chéreau's production, with designs by Richard Peduzzi, emphasized this atmospheric quality by setting it on an enormous stage that dwarfed the actors, with huge metallic walls and doors that slid across the stage hiding one area or opening up another. In this way, the production acquired a cinematic quality that was much commented on by the critics at the time, although many complained that Koltès's play was effectively crushed beneath the monumentalism of the settings.

Maria Casarès performed the role of Cécile and gave an interview in which she was warmly appreciative of Koltès's ability to speak of the marginal zones of modern urban life, giving them an importance that called into question their official marginalization. (See under 'Travel', page 86.)

In the Solitude of the Cotton Fields

This play explores how language may be used as a weapon, to probe, to subdue, to bargain, to lie, to deceive, or to betray. The play contains only two characters, and is prefaced by the paragraph describing what is meant by 'the deal'. (See 'Business and the Deal', page 89.) The characters are named simply The Dealer and The Client, and Koltès said that he imagined the encounter between these two as a duel between two people who would normally do everything possible to avoid one another – for example, the meeting between a Mississippi bluesman and a New York punk.

The duel develops into a trial of strength as the two circle one another, careful to give

nothing away, searching for any weak point in the opponent's defences. This is conflictual dialogue stripped to its bare essentials, with no attempt to supply a realistic setting or motivations for the struggle between the two men. Everything is expressed through insinuation and hidden meanings; no concrete item of exchange is mentioned. Every conceivable *need* is evoked, whether emotional, spiritual, or material, but neither can agree or come to terms.

Despite this, neither can leave: like Vladimir and Estragon in Beckett's *Waiting for Godot*, who long to move on but are unable to do so for reasons that they themselves fail to grasp, Koltès's pair of characters are locked in their antagonistic embrace. The client cannot deny that he has left his home and ventured into the outside world in search of something, and the dealer cannot abandon the attempt to discover what it is that would satisfy his needs.

In the end they can find no common ground that might provide the basis for negotiation, other than the fundamental reality of their conflict or struggle or trial of strength with one another. This reaches its logical conclusion when what began as a purely verbal challenge develops into a duel to the death. The play ends with their joint realization of this reality and the traditional invitation to a duel: 'Choose your weapon.'

Michel Bataillon has pointed out that Koltès's dialogue, while remaining (mostly) down to earth, is steeped in philosophical speculation: 'philosophical dialogues on solitude, on desire, on fear, on the magnetism of love and of hatred, on the eternal laws of commerce' (*Théâtre en Europe*, 18, 1988); and Michael Billington wrote that Chéreau's production (at the 1995 Edinburgh Festival) 'has the visceral power of a heavyweight contest as two men slug it out linguistically in a strange, twilit street encounter' (*The Guardian*, 1 September 1995).

Listening to Koltès's dialogue has a distorting effect on the listener's perception of time, rather similar to that induced by an Andy Warhol film, in which the lighting of a match was made to last for a whole hour. Maybe the meeting of the Dealer and the

Lipstick

Scene 4 from an unfinished play by Bernard-Marie Koltès, 1988. First published in Séquence, 2 (1995), the magazine of the Théâtre National de Strasbourg, and translated by David Bradby.

Coco (Chanel) is lounging in her slip and talking to her maid Consuelo.

COCO   Consuelo, do stop putting on that lipstick; every time you swallow, every time you sigh, you daub on another layer of that horrible paint. Consuelo, I am disgusted by your lipstick.

CONSUELO   Why, Madame, why are you disgusted?

COCO   Lipstick is a horrible invention; it's indecent, it's obscene. Do you imagine it's pretty? Do you think men find it attractive? Do you imagine you are in a position to be able to ignore what men find attractive? A woman who is not attractive to men is nothing, less than nothing. A woman who is not loved by a man is a wash-out. Do you imagine you can attract a man by making yourself look like a cake, or a squashed strawberry, or a red wine stain on a table cloth? Do you think it's pleasant to see cigarette ends in the ashtrays with their filters ringed by that obscene redness?

CONSUELO   I don't smoke, Madame Coco, I never have.

COCO   Even if you don't smoke, the world is full of stubs that are smeared all over with red and then, if you pick them up, you get it all over your fingers.

CONSUELO   I don't pick up cigarette stubs.

COCO   You should, you should; then you'd see what it's like to get it all over your fingers, and then your blouse and then your face. It's all so improper, Consuelo, so terribly improper. Look at all those women who drink in cocktail bars: they think nothing of leaving their glasses with a red peel stuck to the edge. They couldn't care less. They purr like cats who have done their business on the rug; they just put on more lipstick, pushing their lips into a shape like a plughole. Do they really think that men are attracted by drains? Men are disgusted by drains. But those idiotic women don't care, they just go on doing their business.

CONSUELO   I don't go to cocktail bars.

COCO   But at least you wash glasses: that's your job, washing. If you worked in a different house you'd see whether it's easy to remove that red smear which slithers around beneath the sponge. I'll try putting some on the rims of the cups and glasses. I'll go on doing it until you're disgusted too. And in any case, why on earth do you put that revolting paint on your mouth, where it annoys everyone and dirties everything?

Why not put some on your forehead, and on your neck, like the Sioux?

If you really must colour yourself red, at least put it on like war paint. But, please, not on your lips: lips are being used all the time, for all sorts of different purposes. Would you really dare kiss a man, Consuelo, and leave that grotesque mark on his cheek?

Would you do that and then abandon him, having to get rid of the stain? Do you think you have the right to mark men as if you were a cowboy branding cattle?

CONSUELO   I don't kiss men.

COCO   It really doesn't matter whether you kiss them or not. Do you think you have the right to place your stamp on everything that comes near you without disgusting people?

CONSUELO   I never kiss anyone.

COCO   Lipstick is the most vulgar, the most disgusting invention ever thought up to harm women. Consuelo, why do you smear your lips with this repulsive stuff?

CONSUELO   It's like a hem, Madame Coco; like when you make a button-hole. If you don't fold over the edges and sew them up carefully, the hole will get bigger and bigger. I'm afraid of my mouth unravelling and becoming enormous.

COCO   But you have lips, for heaven's sake. That's what they're for. Nobody's mouth has ever unravelled. Your mouth is already well hemmed.

CONSUELO   Not well, Madame Coco, it's not tidy. It frays at the edges. I'm frightened, Madame Coco, that suddenly it will tear at the corner and the whole mouth will split.

COCO   Your fears are insane. And take off those high-heeled shoes. Yet another grotesque invention. Why on earth do women think they need to announce their arrival with a footwear fanfare? Women are so stupid, so stupid. Consuelo, take off those shoes at once: I'm exhausted by their noise.

Client only takes a few seconds, but that brief encounter is expanded by the stating out loud of every thought that passes or might pass through the minds of the two characters. Just as Beckett's plays are made up of dialogue that reminds us of the words that babble incessantly in our heads and are unquenchable, even if we try to silence them, so Koltès's dialogue in this play suggests a perfectly banal encounter, in which the words spoken by the two characters are entirely composed of subtext. In short, we can imagine them saying quite conventional things to one another in reality, but listening to the words on stage is like following every twist and turn in the labyrinth of their subconscious, as every conceivable ramification of their encounter plays itself out.

The original production was by Patrice Chéreau at the Théâtre des Amandiers, Nanterre, in 1987, with the roles being taken by Laurent Malet (The Client) and Isaach de Bankolé (The Dealer). Later the same year, Chéreau revived this production with himself in the role of the Dealer, and it remained in his repertoire until 1990. In 1995, he mounted an entirely new production, with Pascal Greggory as the Client and himself, again, as the Dealer. This was the production that visited the Edinburgh Festival as well as the Venice Biennale, the Madrid Festival de Otono de la Communidad, and the Festival d'Automne in Paris.

It was performed in traverse on a bare stage with a highly imaginative lighting design, and the critics mostly shared Michael Billington's judgement that it was one of the great festival events of the year (*The Guardian*, 1 September 1995). The first time that Chéreau took the role of the Dealer, in October 1987, Koltès had been thoroughly put out, insisting that he had written the role for a black actor. But in time he forgave Chéreau, pleased that the play continued to be performed and to draw audiences.

An English translation by Christopher Rathbone was performed at the Almeida Theatre in 1991, directed by Kim Dambaek. This translation was also given to audiences attending Chéreau's production at the Edinburgh Festival in 1995.

Return to the Desert

In this play, Koltès returned to the main theme of much of his early work: the family, its conflictual relationships, and its links with property, inheritance, ownership. In earlier works such as *L'Héritage* or *Sallinger*, Koltès had used the family as the basic social unit within which both agreement and dissent, belonging and rejection could be expressed. In ways that recall both Faulkner and Salinger, Koltès presents individuals who may feel alienated within the family structure, but who return to it as the only environment in which they can discover self-definition.

The play opens with a pitched battle between Mathilde and her brother Adrien. It is November 1960. Mathilde is 52, Adrien 50. They are the last survivors of a bourgeois family which had made a fortune from the expansion of the Lorraine steel industry in the early years of the century, but can now do nothing to delay its decline, lacking the energy or imagination needed to diversify into other kinds of manufacturing.

Because she never behaved like a proper bourgeoise in her youth, Mathilde was victimized by her brother and his friends; after the Liberation of France in 1945, she was accused of sleeping with the Germans, and paraded through Metz with her hair shaved off. She fled to Algeria to build a new life, where she brought up her two children, Fatima and Edouard. Now she is once again fleeing from hostilities (in Algeria) and returns to confront Adrien in the family home.

The saga of a family dynasty is not new, but the linking of a provincial industrial family to the Algerian war has considerable originality, for while the Second World War and German occupation of France have provided material for hundreds of plays and films, very few dramatists have dealt with the equally disturbing material of the war in Algeria. And yet this war, which lasted from 1954 until 1962 cost over 100,000 dead or wounded, and affected the lives of everyone who lived in France or in its North African colonies.

Koltès never wrote 'issue' plays in the straightforward sense. His method of handling social and political concerns was always oblique. Just as he insisted that *Struggle* was not a play about neocolonialism, so *Return* is not directly about the Algerian war. Rather, it deals with attitudes and social realities which both explain and are explained by the conflict in Algeria. It concerns itself with the mentalities current in the early 1960s in a provincial town such as Metz, and the action of the play develops a rich interweaving of the characters' dreams and aspirations, their behaviour in the private spaces of the home, and their actions in the society outside. In fact a principal theme of the play is how the French managed to deny the reality of the war going on in Algeria. Implied within this is the question of ownership – not only of colonial territories, but of France, of national heritage, of the right to space, both physical and ideological.

The linguistic texture of the play has a condensed, calculated quality, designed to ensure that even the most banal exchanges between the characters bring into play a whole range of cultural and ideological values. Because both the historical and geographical background of the characters is established in such detail, the speeches of the characters are closer to realistic, everyday dialogue than those of some earlier plays. Nevertheless, they retain a strong imprint of their author's original approach to dramatic dialogue: there are many virtuoso passages of monologue, and in many places what is being voiced in the play is clearly their thoughts, anxieties, or nightmares, rather than anything the characters would readily say to one another in ordinary, everyday speech.

The action covers a period of roughly nine months, during which time Adrien and Mathilde squabble over everything as they did when they were children. But now their fighting has a life-and-death seriousness. Through her daughter, Mathilde makes contact again with her dead childhood friend Marie, and becomes convinced that she was murdered by Adrien; she wreaks vengeance on Adrien's friends (who now make up the ruling class in Metz) for their share in her humiliation in 1945; Mathilde's daughter,

Fatima, becomes pregnant in similar circumstances to those of her mother, and gives birth to half-caste twins; finally both sister and brother realize that they have no future in Metz, and they leave together for a life of retirement wandering around the spa towns of the world, forever in exile.

For *Return to the Desert*, Koltès was keen that the premiere should be in central Paris rather than at Nanterre. Much as he admired Chéreau, he felt that his association with him was leading him to be seen as a playwright whose work was 'difficult', and strictly for the rather self-consciously cultivated audience that attended avant-garde theatre. Keen for his plays to appeal to a broader public, he had written the main role of Mathilde specially for Jacqueline Maillan, a popular performer with her own following who specialized in boulevard comedy and seldom appeared in a 'serious' play. Accordingly, the production, directed by Chéreau, and sponsored by the Théâtre des Amandiers, took place at the Théâtre du Rond-Point in the centre of Paris in 1988.

However, the production was not greeted with the same acclaim as *The Night just before the Forests* or *Struggle of the Dogs and the Black*. The comedy in the text was not so successfully realized, and the audience appeared to find the production puzzling. According to Chéreau, this was because Jacqueline Maillan's audience expected a traditional boulevard comedy, and were perplexed by the play, whereas the Nanterre habitués who attended felt that Koltès and Chéreau were selling out.

Koltès himself helped to muddy the waters by complaining about the world premiere of the play in Hamburg, directed by Alexander Lang, accusing it of being *too* lightweight. It was not until Jacques Nichet's revival in 1995 that the play received the comic performance it deserved, and that the critics agreed on the merits of the piece. The role of Mathilde in this production was taken by Myriam Boyer, who had played Léona in the 1983 production of *Struggle of the Dogs and the Black*. An English translation was commissioned by Midnight Theatre Company from David Bradby in

1992. The company's director, Derek Wax, produced a staged reading at the Traverse, Edinburgh, in 1993, with Sian Phillips as Mathilde and Paul Godfrey as Adrien. This translation will be published by Methuen in 1997.

Roberto Zucco

Koltès's anti-hero Roberto Zucco is a character whose mythical dimensions are more outsize than any of his previous dramatic characters. He walks free over the roof of the high security prison in which he had been held; he quotes passages of Victor Hugo; his death is heralded by a hurricane and an explosion in the heavens, 'as blinding as an atomic bomb'. He was described by the author as 'a mythical character, a hero like Samson or Goliath, monsters of strength, finally struck down by a stone or a woman'. And yet, paradoxically, this is also the most realistic of Koltès's plays, in which the dialogue comes closest to everyday speech while nevertheless retaining a certain poetic density.

Koltès first became interested in the case of Roberto Succo in 1988, when he saw a 'wanted' poster on the metro which carried photographs of him. Succo had murdered both parents and had been given a life sentence in Italy in 1981. But after five years he had succeeded in escaping, and had been at liberty for nearly two years, committing a string of other offences, including the murder of a police inspector, before being recaptured.

Back in prison, in Treviso, he gave his guards the slip for long enough to climb onto the prison roof, where he remained for some time, throwing tiles and shouting to the assembled journalists, before being recaptured. Shortly afterwards he committed suicide. Koltès saw the pictures of Succo's final defiant hours on the roof of the prison when they were broadcast on the television news, and was fascinated by the way the media presented him. According to Pascale Froment, the first thing that had struck him about the 'wanted' poster was that it included four different portraits of Succo:

'each one showed a face that was so different from the others that you had to look several times before you could be sure it was the same person' (*Alternatives Théâtrales*, 35- 36, June 1990, p. 41).

Koltès depicts Zucco's life as taking place in a kind of labyrinth, where nothing is quite what it seems. Above all, he offers us a Zucco who never appears quite the same from one scene to the next. Like the photos on the 'wanted' poster, like the images of the real Succo broadcast by the media, each depiction of Zucco is different, depending on the perspective from which he is seen, and the person who is looking.

The play is prefaced by an extract from an ancient ritual of the cult of Mithras, quoted by Jung in the last interview he gave to the BBC, and it manages to combine throughout the action resonances of a mythical and psychoanalytical kind, as well as the brutal realities of the Succo murders. The crimes committed by the central character do not become the subject of an 'investigation' (as in a detective thriller) nor of an explanation (as in a psychological thriller).

In common with some English playwrights such as Edward Bond, Koltès clearly felt that violence was one of the defining features of our society: one that we try not to see and that should not be explained away. The play concerns itself as much with the attitudes towards violence in society as with the monstrous nature of Zucco's actions.

This appears most clearly in Scene 10, one of the most successful, which takes place in a public park. Here Zucco takes hostage a woman and her young son. The dramatization of the episode lays emphasis on the role of the bystanders, their voyeuristic fascination with the events enacted before their eyes, their desire for a juicy crime, and their need to demonize Zucco as the young hooligan. For Peter Stein, the play's first director, this scene shows how, in the television age,

the public needs to 'have an experience'. The poor criminals end up in the role of victims: they become the actors performing, doing a job of work required by everyone else.

Interview in *Alternatives Théâtrales*, p. 53

Top: *Roberto Zucco* (in Russian) with the actors of the Maly Theatre, St Petersburg, directed by Lluis Pasqual, Odéon Théâtre de l'Europe, 1994. Bottom: the same production revived by Lluis Pasqual for the Venice Biennale, 1995. Photos: Ros Ribas.

Each bystander has a different explanation of what is going on, but far from explaining the dilemma of the Woman, the Child, or Zucco, they simply tell us about their own mentalities. Their superficial explanations of criminal conduct remind the audience of the 'rationalizations' of Zucco's behaviour offered by the comic duo who appeared in the first scene as prison warders, and who return in Scene 14 as policemen. One is convinced that every criminal's behaviour is explained by sex, the other that it's just a matter of pure vice. In the reactions of the bystanders, Koltès dramatizes the fascination with violence of contemporary society.

Roberto Zucco received its world premiere in German at the Berlin Schaubühne, directed by Peter Stein, in April 1990, a year after the author's death. Koltès had been keen for Stein to produce the play, having seen and admired his production of Chekhov's *Three Sisters*. Stein said that he had fallen in love with the play, despite not being attracted to Koltès's earlier work. He felt that in *Roberto Zucco* Koltès for the first time had overcome his tendency to write in an excessively literary style, and had created a genuinely dramatic structure.

In the four years following, there were another sixteen new productions of the play in German theatres, and the French premiere, directed by Bruno Boeglin at the Théâtre National Populaire, Villeurbanne, on 7 November 1991, has been followed by several further productions, including one at the Théâtre National de Strasbourg, directed by Jean-Louis Martinelli, in March 1995.

In addition to this, the play has been performed in Austria, Canada, Colombia, Denmark, Spain, Finland, Hungary, Italy, Norway, Holland, Poland, Romania, Russia, Switzerland, the Czech Republic, and Venezuela. The play has yet to receive its first British performance, but in 1995 the Royal Court Theatre commissioned a translation from Martin Crimp: a production is planned (director: James MacDonald), and the translation will be published by Methuen in 1997.

Themes and Preoccupations

Home

For a long time I hoped to experience that emotion of which I had often heard tell: the emotion a man feels on returning home. Of course I had felt something a bit like it, when I came back to Paris after a journey, but that feeling seemed rather silly and superficial, in any case nothing to make a lot of fuss about. One day – I forget where, somewhere far from Paris in a rather hostile environment – suddenly, coming from a bar or a passing car, muffled and distant, I heard a few bars of an old Bob Marley record, and I let out a sort of sigh, just like landowners do in books when they settle into a chair, beside the fire, in the sitting room of their hacienda. And no matter where I am now, if I catch the sounds of *Rat Race* or *War*, even if they are quite distant, I experience the familiar smell, the sense of invulnerability and the repose of home.

Prologue (Minuit, 1991), p. 119

Travel

From an interview with Maria Casarès

I believe that Koltès is a traveller, a wanderer who goes looking into the remotest corners of a town or of the world, the places that are most isolated. I believe that these remote places are set to become the centre of our world. Europe, which has served as a beacon for humanity, has been witness to the extremities of the world coming and setting up home in its centre; and I feel that Koltès places at the centre of his plays everything that was once considered marginal. In reality, the centre has seized up; it is the extremities which are alive, and which are moving into the centre and bringing life to it. . . .

Koltès speaks to us of things we did not know, or of things that we know, but which are revealed as new, while at the same time awaking memories of what is most ancient (like the Quechua language in *Quai Ouest*).

Further scenes from the production of *Roberto Zucco*, Odéon Théâtre de l'Europe, 1994. Photos: Ros Ribas.

If we are to succeed in performing him, in producing his work fully, we still have much to discover. This is true of both actors and directors. Koltès is of our time, but I also feel that he is a writer who is ahead of our time: he seems to have written after our time.

Maria Casarès, interviewed while working on *Quai ouest*, reprinted in *Alternatives Théâtrales*, 35-36 (June 1990), p. 25-8

The Stage

I see the stage rather as a temporary space which the characters are constantly trying to get away from. It's like a place where you would say to yourself: this isn't real life, so what do I need to do to escape from it? Any solution always presents itself as having to be played out offstage, rather like in classical theatre.

For my generation, more used to cinema than to theatre, the symbol for the reverse of stage space might be the automobile: speed, constant change of place, etc. And the challenge for theatre becomes: how to get away from the stage and rediscover real life. It must, of course be understood that I have no idea whether real life exists anywhere and if, when they finally get off stage, the characters don't find themselves on another stage, in another theatre, and so on. This is perhaps the one essential question which allows the theatre to survive.

I have always rather detested theatre, since theatre is the opposite of life; but I always come back to it, and I love it because it is the one place where you say: this is not life.

'Un hangar, à l'ouest', reprinted in *Roberto Zucco* (Minuit, 1990)

Actors

Actors are always too slow. They have this tendency not to speak the words, but to weigh them, to show them, to give them meaning. In fact a text should always be spoken like a child who recites a lesson with a desperate desire to pee, who goes very fast, shifting from one leg to the other and, when it is finished, rushes out to do it.

An actor should never try to deduce the characters' psychology from what they say; on the contrary, the characters should be made to speak according to what the actor has deduced of their being from their actions.

'Pour mettre en scène *Quai ouest*', in *Quai ouest* (Minuit, 1985), p. 104

Africa

Struggle of the Dogs and the Black speaks neither of Africa nor of Blacks – I am not an African author – it is not about neo-colonialism nor the racial question. It certainly presents no opinions.

It simply speaks of a place in the world. It sometimes happens that you come across a place which is a kind of metaphor for life or for an aspect of life, or for something which presents itself to me as both serious and obvious, such as Conrad's rivers running up into the jungle. . . . I had spent a month visiting friends on a public works project in Africa. Imagine, out in the bush, a little citadel of five or six houses surrounded by barbed wire with watch towers; and inside, a dozen or so whites living in a state of terror at what lay outside, with black guards, armed and posted all around. It was only shortly after the end of the Biafran war and gangs of pillagers were roaming the region. To prevent themselves falling asleep during the night, the guards would call to one another, uttering strange throaty cries. . . . They reverberated all night long. That is what made me decide to write this play, the cries of the guards. And the fact that inside this circle the people were acting out the same petit-bourgeois dramas that you might find in the seizième arrondissement of Paris: the project leader was sleeping with the foreman's wife, things like that. . . .

My play speaks, perhaps, of France and of whites: when you see something from a distance or from an unfamiliar place, it sometimes becomes easier to interpret. The play speaks, above all, of three human beings isolated in a part of the world that is foreign to them, surrounded by enigmatic guards. I thought – and I still think – that to recount the cries of these guards, heard in the depths of Africa, the area of anxiety and solitude that they stake out, was a subject of some importance.

Afterword to *Combat de nègre et de chiens*, printed on the back of the Minuit edition

Business and 'the Deal'

I have never liked love stories. They don't tell you very much. I don't believe in the love relationship in itself. It was an invention of the Romantics. . . . If you want to tell a story with any subtlety you have to take a different route. I consider the 'deal' to be a sublime means. It encompasses everything else. It would be good to be able to write a play where the action is between a man and a woman and is entirely to do with 'business'.

Quoted by Michel Bataillon, in *Théâtre en Europe*, No.18 (Sept. 1988), p. 26

Epigraph to
'In the Solitude of the Cotton Fields'

A *deal* is a commercial transaction concerning values that are banned or subject to strict controls, and which is conducted in neutral spaces, indeterminate and not intended for this purpose, between suppliers and consumers, by means of tacit agreement, conventional signs, or conversations with double meanings – whose aim is to circumvent the risks of betrayal or swindle implicit in this kind of operation – at any time of day or night, with no reference to the regulation opening hours for officially registered trading establishments, but usually at times when the latter are closed.

This explanation of 'the deal', written in a parody of bureaucratic language, suggests a very Balzacian view of society, peopled by individuals all governed by the feverish need to buy and sell. In addition, it expresses this in terms that are deeply coloured by our late twentieth-century awareness of commerce as a global entity with a life of its own, often secretive or underhand and constantly eluding official attempts to control it.

But Koltès's description of the deal goes beyond such obvious references, also suggesting something about the transactional communication that is theatre. For if Koltès's view of society bears comparison with Balzac's, his literary method is closer to the neoclassical discipline of Racine than to the sprawling, encyclopedic quality of the nineteenth-century novelist. Koltès's paragraph neatly identifies the fundamental quality shared by any dramatic dialogue or situation: it is a tension arising from an encounter between two people, each of whom wants something from the other, each of whom is using words transactionally, i.e., is seeking to do something to the other in and through the words that are spoken.

Capoeira

Because they were not permitted to bear arms, slaves in Brazil invented a martial art; today this form of contest is still taught and practised, but in it the combatants never touch one another; their skill consists in coming within a hair's breadth of an opponent, making passes to music; the art is taught in the academies of Salvador and Bahia, and is performed for the tourists in Rio.

One day, on a public square, I saw two combatants, one of whom, whether by mistake or by design, struck the other. Then they began to lay into one another in earnest; the crowd protested, then went off in disgust. Each man set about slugging it out in high style, with no rules and no musical accompaniment, until both were unconscious, in the middle of the square, on their own.

Prologue (Minuit, 1991), p. 116

The Author Present in the Text

Heiner Müller on the plays of Koltès
(Müller translated *Quai ouest* into German)

His texts are tremendous because of the way they combine Rimbaud and Faulkner. His characters are constructed and developed on the basis of language alone. At the same time you can find a Molièresque structure in Koltès's texts. This Molièresque structure, made up of a set of arias, emerges most clearly in *Le Retour au désert*. Doubtless this has something to do with the subject: the French family into which something makes a sudden violent entry. What Koltès achieves is something very rare in recent dramatic writing. Many playwrights structure their work solely around a plot, and plot in the theatre is boring. It's much better to have an obscure plot or to break away from the plot structure completely. Koltès, on the other hand, uses an 'aria' structure. That means that the author is more or less present in his own texts and characters. That seems to me to be very important, because at the moment there is a tendency to expel the author from the text and from the theatre as well. That's the fundamental reason why Koltès is the only new playwright to interest me.

From 'Aucun texte n'est à l'abri du théâtre', interview with Heiner Müller, *Alternatives Théâtrales*, 35-36 (June 1990), p. 12

On Returning to Koltès's Work

After the death of Koltès, I stopped working on his plays. I could have put on *Roberto Zucco* but I did not, because, in a way, the death of Bernard Koltès had put a stop to the work I was doing with him: it was work with a living author, which is quite different from the work you do on a dead author, or one from the past. So, for five years, I stopped reading his plays or working on them – especially since Bernard had himself asked me not to direct *Roberto Zucco*, because he wanted it to be put on by a different director, Luc Bondy at first, and then Peter Stein.

I think that was because Koltès had felt divided: he was very pleased for me to put on his plays, especially since I directed four of them one after the other, but at the same time he felt rather stifled, limited by the fact that, once I had put on one of his plays, no one else in France dared to touch it. There were also difficulties that arose from the critical reception of his plays. When the French critics first discovered Koltès, they thought one of two things: either that he had not written them alone – that we wrote them together, or that I collaborated in the writing of them, which was quite untrue; or that there was a total identification between his world and mine – which was not true either.

So, I waited five years before putting on a Koltès play again, and before re-reading *Dans la solitude des champs de coton*, so as to be able to see, to hear, how it resonated within me and what I could hear in it, and whether it would be possible for me to come up with a completely different reading of it – one that would be, in a way, unfaithful to what Koltès used to tell me when he was there, but more faithful, in a profound sense, to what he had written, even to what he had written without knowing it.

It can be very difficult to follow faithfully and to keep step with an author as he is in the process of creating himself; when you admire him deeply, you sometimes find it difficult to be a little bit unfaithful to him. You can be very intimidated. The difference between the production I did eight years ago and today's production is that I am no longer intimidated by Bernard Koltès, since he is no longer there. In 1987, I was very much intimidated by him.

The moment comes when, in order to be genuinely faithful to him, to get right to the bottom of his ideas, you have to be a little bit unfaithful to him, and it's very difficult to be unfaithful to a living author. The example with which I identify most closely is that of Stanislavski and Chekhov. As everyone knows, Chekhov was not pleased, most of the time, with Stanislavski's productions of his plays; but, at the same time, without Stanislavski, Chekhov would not perhaps have had the same impact.

Patrice Chéreau,
interviewed by David Bradby, 1995

NTQ Book Reviews

edited by Maggie Gale

Theatre History to 1900

James Morwood and David Crane, eds.
Sheridan Studies
Cambridge: Cambridge University Press, 1995.
ISBN 0-521-46466-8.

This volume claims to be the 'first systematic attempt to establish Sheridan as a major figure in the history of English comedy'. The claim is quite misleading. The book consists of essays written by a variety of individuals examining different facets of Sheridan's career – there is nothing systematic about the choice or content of the essays, and the quality fluctuates widely.

In structural terms the book offers an impressionistic view of Sheridan the man and of his work as writer and politician. Most of the contributors have either written books on or edited works by Sheridan. With some notable exceptions their essays for this volume read like a collection of afterthoughts. The exceptions include Jack Durant's finely crafted piece 'Sheridan and Language', Christopher Reid's penetrating analysis of 'Argument and Identity in Sheridan's Speeches', and Marc Baer's detailed and convincingly illustrated account of 'The Rise and Fall of Sheridan as Political Reformer'.

Closing the volume is an interview with the director Peter Wood – who, with elegiac nostalgia, recalls his production of *The Rivals* 'before the dark time of deconstructive thinking . . . militant feminism, and political correctness engulfed our culture'. He goes on to comment perceptively on the warmth of characterization in *The Rivals* in contrast to the chilling nature of *The School for Scandal*.

DAVID THOMAS

John Peacock
The Stage Designs of Inigo Jones:
the European Context
Cambridge: Cambridge University Press, 1995.
xxii, 387 p. £75.00.
ISBN 0-521-41812-7.

This profusely illustrated, beautifully produced book is a wide-ranging study of Inigo Jones as a stage designer. Its amply documented thesis is that Jones was indebted to the notion of 'imitation' not only in his commitment to an Aristotelian aesthetic of mimesis but also in his

lifelong habit of 'copying' from the works of his mainly Italian masters and models in the effort to educate both himself and his courtly audiences. To imitate nature, Jones believed, it was necessary to imitate art, in architecture and in stage design.

John Peacock considers all the major areas of Jones's activity as a designer. He sheds light on his collaboration with Ben Jonson and the reasons for its dissolution. He brings out the extent to which Jones's designs of buildings were copies of the Italians, and at the same time how much the scenic architecture in his designs for masques and courtly entertainments was a vital part of his education as an architect of real buildings when he became Surveyor of the King's Works. Peacock also provides detailed consideration of the resources at Jones's disposal in designing a figurative repertory for the masquers and their more extravagant professional foils, the antimasquers; in creating landscapes and the proscenium arches themselves; and in representing antiquity in the masques.

In his closing pages the author reflects interestingly on the parallels between Jones's exaltation of Stuart absolutism and his own aesthetic dominance as a reforming designer, once he had successfully ended his long rivalry with Jonson. Apart from its scholarly detail there is much here to stimulate the non-specialist student of theatre who wishes to know and think more about the revolution in ways of seeing and understanding the world which occurred in the English theatre mainly because of Jones's work.

BRIAN CROW

Amelia Howe Kritzer, ed.
Plays by Early American Women, 1775-1850
Ann Arbor: University of Michigan Press, 1995.
ISBN 0-472-06598-X.

Having been forced to decipher several of these plays from 1960s reader-opaque micro cards on an antiquated reader in the British Library, I can give a heartfelt welcome to Kritzer's republication of them in an accessible edition. Apart from Mary Otis Warren's *The Group* (1775), they have all long been unavailable. Its revolutionary satire sets the tone for those who followed in celebrating American nationalism and beginning to explore what it might mean for women.

Mary Carr Clarke's *The Fair Americans* (1815) looks critically at the war of 1812 against Canada from the point of view of the women left behind, examining its tedium, economic consequences, and encouragement of male self-aggrandisement. Even Sarah Pogson Smith's 1807 *The Female Enthusiast*, about Charlotte Corday, manages to introduce America – as a place where, 'Each female who respects herself is safe', an alternative space where perhaps the uneasy dilemmas of imagining a heroine who takes political action through the ultimate transgression of murder can be resolved.

The discourse of nationalism and feminism is often problematic. The heroine of Susanna Rowson's *Slaves of Algiers* (1794) comes 'from that land where virtue in either sex is the only mark of superiority', but like other works of the period, while borrowing the imagery of slavery to describe women's subjugation and enacting a plot of women snatched by 'surly Orientals', it completely fails to acknowledge the existence of actual slavery in 'the land of the free'. The most interesting play in the volume is *Altorf* (1819), by Frances Wright, who emigrated from Scotland to join Robert Owen's New Harmony community: this opens with a preface celebrating republican liberty, and uses the story of the rebellion of the Swiss cantons against their overlords to explore radical revolt, but movingly examines the personal costs of political convictions and loyalties.

SUSAN CROFT

Twentieth-Century Theatre

Charlotte Canning
Feminist Theatres in the USA:
Staging Women's Experience
London; New York: Routledge, 1996. £12.99.
ISBN 0-415-09805-X.

The feminist student of theatre and the feminist theatre practitioner will find valuable material in Canning's study of the explosion of feminist theatre groups and theatre making in the USA from the late 1960s to the mid 1980s. Canning opens with overviews of early critical approaches to the feminist theatre movement – useful to the reader who is less familiar with the field of feminist theatre, or does not have access to these early studies – and moves to detailing the experiences of women working in experimental theatre groups, and how, in turn, this created a need for women to inaugurate their own companies.

Particular attention is paid to the work of four groups, chosen because they have received relatively little published recognition: the Women's Experimental Theater, Spiderwoman Theater,

Lilith, and Front Room Theater Guild. Two chapters devoted to productions are less convincing because they run into the difficulty of presenting descriptive accounts of past performance events which the reader is unlikely to have seen. 'The Community as Audience' as a feature of feminist practice is, however, a much more rewarding chapter, and a useful addition to the growing body of work which takes the spectator as its focus.

The study makes excellent use of interviews as oral history, which keeps the collective rather than the individual in focus, and allows the reader access to the tensions and behind-the-scenes arguments. Given that funding is crucial to the inception and life of any theatre company, as a British reader I would have found contextualization of the American funding system and more detail on the specific funding of women's theatre helpful. As issues of gender and performance are currently so important to the field of theatre studies, it would be good to see Routledge commissioning many more volumes in this valuable series.

ELAINE ASTON

Susan Painter
Edgar the Playwright
London: Methuen, 1996. xx, 202 p. £9.99.
ISBN 0-413-69960-9.

This, the latest in Methuen's somewhat intermittent series, is, surprisingly, only the second full-length study of David Edgar's work to be published. As such it sets itself the clear intention of dealing both chronologically and thematically with what it is argued are the most important works of his career to date, culminating with an account of one of the most impressive, *Pentecost* (1994). With her conscious decision not to deal, other than very generally – as with her account of Edgar's early work with General Will, for instance – with unpublished plays, Susan Painter is aiming at a general theatregoing audience as well as a student readership, for whom the accessibility of texts is everything.

Running through the thread of her always incisive analysis of the plays is an account of the changes and developments in the playwright's own political thinking, seen always as vitally connected with the changes and developments in his dramatic models. Indeed, Painter rightly allows Edgar to speak for himself all the way through her account, drawing from his vast catalogue of journalistic writings and from her own interviews.

Edgar is a playwright for whom the processes of research are all important, both in the creation of the text and, as Painter frequently makes clear, of the production. The play becomes a part of the process of education for writer, production team, cast, and audience alike; and to see this process traced through the writer's career is to be taken into many of the crucial debates about the relationship between politics and the theatre in contemporary Britain from the late 1960s on.

Painter is not frightened to enter the lists of controversy – in particular over Edgar's magnificent appropriation of the new Barbican space in the 1980s with *Maydays*, a play that was, perhaps understandably if wrongly, attacked from both the left and the right – but is always careful to present the evidence for both the prosecution and the defence.

Edgar's move away from what he describes as his late 1960s position is traced and placed within the context of larger changes on the left and in society as a whole, in Britain and in a post-'Iron Curtain' Europe that has come to interest Edgar increasingly in, for instance, *The Shape of the Table* and *Pentecost*; so that a central theme in his work from *Maydays* on can be seen to be a squaring-up to the full implications of the unfulfilled revolutionary dreams of Eastern Europe.

There will be much more to be written about the work of a playwright who is now firmly established as a major figure both nationally and internationally – and there will undoubtedly be many more plays to write about; but Susan Painter provides a lucid and succinct account of Edgar's work which argues well for the need to see his work as an exciting and developing continuum, of vital importance in a modern world that needs the kind of constant interrogation that only a playwright of his stature can offer.

JOHN BULL

Jean Benedetti
The Moscow Art Theatre Letters
London: Methuen, 1995. 377 p. £12.99.
ISBN 0-413-9870-X.

The welcome publication in paperback of Jean Benedetti's selections from the correspondence between leading players involved in the legendary Moscow Art Theatre will doubtless make even more accessible, particularly to students of theatre, first-hand accounts of rehearsal, production preparation, and performance over an extraordinary forty-year span from 1897 to 1938.

Benedetti has grouped the correspondence into four parts, each prefaced by a short but helpful introduction to the period covered. The first part is a brief prologue which documents the origins of the theatre, specifically communication between Stanislavski and Nemirovich-Danchenko that followed their famous June 1897 meeting at Slavyanski Bazar, through which the co-founders grapple with the practicalities of their planned endeavour, the financial, managerial, and artistic details which were to become the source of

considerable contention and disagreement in future years.

The second, and most substantial, part contains correspondence over the first decade of the theatre's work, providing a gold-mine of information, particularly on the often acutely temperamental and sensitive relationship of Anton Chekhov to a new theatre desperate to secure his sure-fire box office plays before their rivals at the long-established Maly could get their hands on them. Invaluable insights into MAT's productions of *Uncle Vanya*, *Three Sisters*, and *The Cherry Orchard* are all provided through correspondence between Chekhov, Nemirovich, Stanislavski, Olga Knipper, Meyerhold, Gorki, and others.

The third part traces the inevitable power struggles that were to emerge from the summer of 1904 onwards after Chekhov's death from tuberculosis and Nemirovich's flat refusal to accept Gorki as natural playwriting heir at the theatre. Here also are contemporary (mixed) views on Stanislavski's developing system. The final part traces the fate of the theatre in post-revolutionary Russia, following the American tour of 1923 and the suppression of artistic freedom that the Stalinist era was to bring. This is essential reading for anyone remotely interested in twentieth-century theatre.

CHRIS BANFIELD

Howard Brenton
Hot Irons
London: Nick Hern Books, 1995. 272 p. £15.99.
ISBN 1-85459-123-1

This book is essentially intended for fans of Howard Brenton. Part I comprises a series of articles and lectures which he has 'rewritten here and there' for publication. Part II, diaries – of his travels round Britain reading *Romans in Britain*, his travels to Queensland and the Soviet Union, and during rehearsals for the Royal Court production of *Berlin Bertie*. Neither hard-hitting nor provocative, the book's overall impression is of what a good man Brenton is. One is left with the image of a man whose genuine compassion is central to his avowed commitment to political change. However, he doesn't manage to engage the reader with this commitment, or to extend the content beyond himself.

Brenton is surprisingly uncritical of his own work in retrospect. He offers little illuminating perspective, seeming to assume without question that the plays have manifested his original intentions. Students seeking insight into the plays will find little assistance, though they will gain the sense of being party to some of his thoughts as he worked on them. Similarly, although there are occasionally sharp, suggestive insights in the essays, they are undeveloped, their incipient relevances lost as the writer sloughs off possible implications to retreat to the succour of generalized optimism. Of special note is his heartfelt recommendation of Oliver's poem *Penniless Politics*.

Of course it is interesting to read the ruminations of a writer whose work one has admired, and Brenton writes well, sometimes with an engaging self-irony. His thoughtfulness regarding his readings of *Romans in Britain* also offers interesting perspectives on the act of performance. On the whole, however, the book is disappointing, offering neither insights into his work nor any development of his ideas beyond general suggestions. A disappointing volume both for the student and the aficionado: a little more iron and a lot more heat might have hit the mark.

ELAINE TURNER

Brian Cox
The Lear Diaries
London: Methuen, 1995. £12.99.
ISBN 0-413-69880-7.

This is Hall's *Diaries* meets *The Year of the King*, a glum day-by-day record of Cox's thoughts as he rehearsed the Royal National Theatre *Lear* and *Richard III* (with Ian McKellen) and toured from Tokyo to Broadmoor. Around him Thatcher is deposed and the Gulf War rages, and Cox gives the impression that he would rather be anywhere, doing anything, rather than this – most of all, he would rather be in Russia, reliving the events of his earlier, more positive and revealing, *Salem to Moscow*.

Cox is a good travel writer – the pages on theatre in Eastern Europe are especially strong – but he gives a muddy impression of rehearsals with Deborah Warner and Richard Eyre. Probably because his work is intuitive and reactive, there is nothing to compare with Sher's quest for Richard and the experience seems to have been profoundly unhappy for him. This utterly honest book – he explains he wrote it to pay for a new kitchen – is based on tape recordings, and works best when most front-line and instantaneous. It will never lure anyone into the profession, but should be read for its picture of a national company dependent on fixing international deals and pleasing sponsors.

TONY HOWARD

Valerie Grove
Dear Dodie: the Life of Dodie Smith
London: Chatto and Windus, 1996. £20.00.
ISBN 0-701-15753-4.

This, the first authorised biography of Dodie Smith, is a welcome addition to the slowly growing collection of new works on mid twentieth-century playwrights and theatre practitioners. Grove's book is no substitute for Dodie Smith's own autobiographical works, which cover the years of her success in the West End, but it does provide substantial insight into her post-war failure to reintegrate with the theatre world.

Grove has made extensive use of Smith's archives, pointing out that her diaries and journals form a 'magnum opus' which in terms of size puts her plays and novels into the realms of 'mere trifles'. Thus, although the book does not focus entirely on Dodie Smith's theatrical career, it gives vital and detailed information on her many friendships with theatre people – particularly her manic correspondence with and critiques of John Van Druten and her friendship with Christopher Isherwood.

Grove encourages the reader to take Smith seriously as a literary and intellectual figure – and she was a writer who wrote and wrote. Equally, the book reveals Smith's own struggles with the down-side of success – her everlasting disappointment at not repeating her 1930s West End triumphs, and the felt frustrations at the lack of recognition for work produced between *I Capture the Castle* and *101 Dalmatians* and after. This book is a must for anyone interested in women playwrights and in twentieth-century British theatre.

MAGGIE GALE

Performance, Theory, General Studies

David Graver
The Aesthetics of Disturbance:
Anti-Art in Avant-Garde Drama
Ann Arbor: University of Michigan Press, 1995.
ISBN 0-472-10507-8.

The introductory chapters of this book make a lucid distinction between the 'avant-garde' and the 'modernist' projects, the former being an attempt to expand the domain as well as the very conception of art in novel ways, while the latter is a resistance to and critique of the existing dominant culture, otherwise known as bourgeois culture. Five types of avant-garde are defined so as to specify that the most anti-art type of them all has nothing to do with socio-cultural or political objectives or even commentary (as occurs, say, with the surrealists), and is, in fact, a matter of what might best be described as gratuitous action and pure provocation (my terms).

It is precisely this complete and apparently disinterested break with established art, whether bourgeois or modernist, that constitutes the essence of the aesthetics of disturbance which propels the anti-art avant-garde. The major exponents in drama of such an aesthetics are, according to Graver, Oskar Kokoschka, Gottfried Benn, Raymond Roussel, Roger Vitrac, and Wyndham Lewis, each of whom receives a chapter, the author noting that their dramatic output is nevertheless small (Vitrac arguably excepted). Not enough detail is given of their little-known pieces, nor does the information given fully relay what is going on – that is, what the disturbance is.

Among useful insights are those to do with Rousselian collage, which develop the differences between collage and montage explained earlier in the book and allow readers to grasp better the idea of event (another characteristic of the anti-art avant-garde) as distinct from that of art work – the mainstay of modernism, however opposi-tional. For a select audience.

MARIA SHEVTSOVA

Phil Jones
Drama as Therapy: Theatre as Living
London; New York: Routledge, 1996. 326p. £15.99. ISBN 0-415-09970-6.

This book has undertaken a mammoth task in providing an overview of the history, theory, and practice of dramatherapy. As such it is clear and methodical in its approach, signalling what is to come and executing it in a consistent manner with the use of 'plates', 'figures', 'boxes', 'tables', and 'case studies', each listed in separate indexes. There is a useful guide to how to use the book at the beginning which outlines the four parts – definitions, forms, and formats of dramatherapy; history; core processes; theory and practice. This clarity of structure makes the book indispensable to the trainee dramatherapist as a guide to the processes of the discipline, and its integrated approach makes it essential reading for all dramatherapists.

It is moreover, accessible for practitioners and academics who perhaps have knowledge of drama but no background in clinical work or psycho-therapeutic practice, particularly as innumerable examples of clinical practice are provided. How-ever, some aspects of the book will be frustrating for theatre scholars. Precisely because it attempts to cover so much ground, drawing on drama-therapy's eclectic knowledge base, the references to theatre are generalized. Major theatre inno-vators are touched on without sufficient com-parison between their contexts and historical periods, and Jones's definitions of 'theatre' and 'drama' emerge out of a limited discussion of potential meanings.

In this sense the book is more focused on 'dramatic' rather than 'theatrical' process. Very few plays or writers are mentioned, and there is little reference to contemporary theatre practice.

Jones's definitions of the 'core processes of dramatherapy' such as 'personification and im-personation' are sometimes difficult because the terms have meanings in other critical contexts. However, despite these criticisms, I recommend this book for anyone interested in the important and still emergent field of dramatherapy.

ANNA SEYMOUR

Harold B. Segel
Pinocchio's Progeny
Johns Hopkins University Press, 1995. 372 p. £14.00. ISBN 0-801-85262-5.

Segel demonstrates a clear strand through Euro-pean theatre from 1890 to 1935 which focuses on the puppet, used in the broadest sense to indicate marionettes, inanimate objects, automata, and the puppet-like manifestations of such characters as Ubu. The passion for puppets is located in a modernist quest not only to revive the conven-tional theatre through an idealized notion of the physical expressivity of the inanimate object, but moreover to serve as a metaphor for the de-humanization technology can cause. This pup-pet's-eye view comes sparklingly alive when Segel analyzes the plays of both Ghelderode and Lorca, but detailed textual references to puppet-like behaviour within a wide selection of key texts start to become a little pedestrian.

The book covers much of Europe with due regard for Eastern European traditions, on which Segel is a recognized authority. It is therefore no surprise that the Epilogue reaches into the post-war period with a short analysis of Kantor's obsession with the mechanical and the 'dead' double. Yet Segel clearly argues that in spite of the likes of Kantor and Heiner Müller, the fascination with puppets has not been sustained beyond the modernist period.

This book adds historical depth to current debates following the resurgence of interest in 'physical theatre' and the body, at a time when notions of performing are still being challenged by new technologies and virtual reality. With its almost bibliographical detail providing a valuable research resource, it will have strong appeal to specialists.

PAUL ALLAIN

Richard Schechner
The Future of Ritual
London; New York: Routledge, 1995. £12.99. ISBN 0-415-04690-4.

The Future of Ritual is aimed at 'anyone interested in performance, anthropology or Schechner's own work'. 'What the book was performance has become', Schechner states on the first page in a masterly word-dance around the complexities of performance writing. What follows is a mass of references, links, examples taken from his own 'library' of transformed behaviour.

Unlike Barba, for Schechner performance is everywhere: in the street, in Tiananmen Square, in an Indian village. 'Live performance increasingly happens not as art but as religious practice, political demonstration, popular entertainment, sports match, or intimate face to face encounter.' He is careful as ever to say exactly what he is doing, and thus the chapters in this book 'examine various cultural and artistic performances as Jayanganesh Richard Schechner experienced them, thought about them, and was able to put his thoughts into words'. Such precision about the process of writing about performance is enough to make this book compulsory reading for anyone working in the field.

In some ways Richard Schechner is to performance what Richard Dawkins is to biology, with one major difference: performance has no Darwin. No one is more aware of this than Schechner himself, and the very title *The Future of Ritual* poses an evolutionary question to which there is no answer. In place of an overall theory Schechner uses his own passion for human transformation and experience. 'At some point in their history people began performing their dreams', he writes at the end of the book. The anthropologist has put down his note book and has started to dance. Another transformation.

BARRY EDWARDS

Diana Taylor and Juan Villegas, eds.
Negotiating Performance: Gender, Sexuality, and Theatricality in Latin/o America
Durham and London: Duke University Press, 1994. £17.95.
ISBN 0-822-31515-7.

Differing from the majority of studies of Hispanic theatre, which tend to be organized around geographical perimeters, *Negotiating Performance* is a welcome recognition of the plurality of culture commonly referred to under the term Hispanic. The editors have put together a varied and eclectic number of essays on multiple aspects of Latino performance encompassing installations, carnival, transvestism, political demonstrations, Mayan theatre, and playwriting.

Although the essays interrogate numerous subjects, from Juan Flore's intriguing discussion of the exhibit 'Las Casitas', modelled on the houses springing up in the Puerto Rican neighbourhoods of New York, to Jorge Huerta's analysis of the place of Chicanos within the mainstream, certain issues around language and identity recur. The conceptual artist Guillermo Gómez-Peña brilliantly articulates the need to draft a new cultural topography in his provocative open letter to the national Arts Community. Numerous contributors question Latino artists' appropriation of public spaces by individuals as different as the Mexican performer-director Jesufa Rodríguez, media artist Daniel Martínez, and Argentina's Madres de la Plaza de Mayo.

The interview with Jesufa Rodríguez, Kirsten F. Nigro's essay on Mexican women playwrights, and Judith Bettelheim's on the history and politics of Cuban carnival show an awareness of the problems raised by using Anglo-American and French feminist theory to debate 'Third World' cultural production.

Unfortunately Sue-Ellen Case's article, despite effectively addressing, in parts, Chicana-lesbian writing, fails fully to address this issue, too often failing to problematize her own position, and reinforcing rather than deconstructing negative stereotypes. This is not to deny the sophistication of her argument, rather to question the uneasy mixture of 'high' theory and confessional anecdotes used to justify problematic arguments. Bearing in mind the pioneering nature of this volume, one questions the presence of Anglo-American critics such as Case over the many Latino artists and critics currently working in North America.

MARIA M. DELGADO

Printed in the United States
By Bookmasters